MUHLENBERG LIE

NATURAL GAS PRODUCER REGULATION AND TAXATION

NATURAL GAS PRODUCER REGULATION AND TAXATION

Interaction between Federal Producer
Regulation and State Severance Taxation

Milton Russell

and

Laurence Toenjes

1971
MSU Public Utilities Papers
*Institute of Public Utilities
Division of Research
Graduate School of Business Administration
Michigan State University
East Lansing, Michigan*

The Institute of Public Utilities, Graduate School of Business Administration, Michigan State University, publishes books, monographs, and occasional papers as part of its program of promoting academic interest in the study of public utilities and regulation. The views and opinions expressed in these works are solely those of the authors, and acceptance for publication does not constitute endorsement by the Institute, its member companies, or Michigan State University.

ISBN: 0-87744-108-1
Library of Congress Catalog Card Number: 78-635475

**To
Pat and Ann**

Contents

List of Tables   ix
List of Figures   xi
Preface   xiii
1 State Production Taxes and Federal Regulation   1
  Market Imperfection Rationale for Regulation   2
  Time Preference Rationale   3
  Plan of Study   5
2 The Natural Gas Industry and Federal Regulation   6
  FPC Ceiling Price Determination   8
  The "Price" of Natural Gas at the Wellhead   11
  The Relationship between Ceiling and Equilibrium Prices   12
  Observed Ceiling-Equilibrium Price Relationship   16
3 The Field Market Model   20
4 Tax Strategy to Fulfill Posited Goals   24
  Goal 1: Maximization of Intrastate Consumption   25
  Goal 2: Maximization of Total Revenue   26
  Goal 3: Maximization of Tax Revenue   32
  Goal 4: Maximization of Interstate Tax Revenue   34
  Producing State Goals and Optimal Severance Taxes   40
5 Optimal Tax Determination: Texas and Louisiana   42
  Calculation of the Estimates   43
  Results of the Calculations   44
6 Optimal Tax Determination: Common Interstate Market   55
7 Conclusions and Policy Implications   61
  Effect of Severance Tax Increases   62
  The Severance Tax as an Allocative Device   64
  Possible Regulatory Response to Tax Optimization   65
  Policy Interaction and Goal Conflicts   67
Appendix 1   69
Appendix 2   73

vii

List of Tables

IA 48-49

IB 50-51

IIA 52

IIB 53

1 75

2 76-77

3 78

4 79

List of Figures

1	13
2	14
3	15
4	21
5	22
6	25
7	27
8	33
9	35
10	44
11	45
12	47
13	56
14	57
15	58
16	62
17	67

Preface

This study of the relationship between producing state severance taxes and the regulation of the field price of natural gas by the Federal Power Commission is an outgrowth of a larger study dealing with the whole range of costs to the producers (recognized in setting the regulated price) which do not flow to the owners of the reproducible factors of production.

We have limited ourselves to analysis of only one phase of the whole energy question—the interaction between federal natural gas producer regulation and state natural gas severance taxation. By rigorously restricting ourselves to this theme, we hope we have made some contribution to the understanding of the limits within which these separate governmental units can operate. By implication, at least, we also have illuminated other situations where actions by one independent governmental body alter the opportunities of other units to promote different, and perhaps conflicting, ends. This concentration purely on regulatory-taxation interaction has meant the sacrifice of any discussion of the broader policy issues in producer regulation. The relative abundance in the literature of the latter and paucity of the former perhaps justify our choice.

This work was written with several audiences in mind, and our intention was to communicate directly with all of them. For example, in each case where mathematical formulation is used, an explicit effort is made to provide sufficient explanation so that the reader can pass over the mathematics with little loss in understanding, although at some cost in precision. The field market model is presented in both a geometric and a mathematical form to aid in this clarifying process. The institutional formulation is similarly a compromise and suffers accordingly; persons totally unacquainted with the issues may find too little detail is presented to satisfy their needs, while those with some sophistication may regard portions of the description as unnecessary, although we hope not tedious. The policy importance of some of the issues brought out here justifies, in our minds, our perhaps cumbersome attempts to make the analysis directly accessible to diverse groups, including noneconomists.

A caution should be issued at this point, especially to the nonprofessional reader. The important contributions of this study are to be found in its analysis, under restrictive assumptions, of certain variables' directions of change in response to given policy actions. The quantitative results we report from the application of the models are merely illustrative and should be interpreted as indicative only of orders of magnitude. Imprecise data, the restrictiveness of the assumptions, and the generality of the models preclude any greater precision. It should be noted, however, that knowledge of probable directions of change and rough quantitative indications are often sufficient for policy action. Although the decision maker would prefer more information he must sometimes act on even less.

The authors have shared in most phases of the work, but each has contributed more in some areas of expertise than in others. In particular, Laurence Toenjes has borne most of the burden of working out the mathematical formulation of the field market model on which much of this study is based.

The original research was conducted in 1967-1968 under a grant by the Institute of Public Utilities, Graduate School of Business Administration, Michigan State University. Further work has been done under the auspices of the Business Research Bureau and Department of Economics, Southern Illinois University, Carbondale. In the almost two years since the completion of this study the authors have been able to test its implications. We believe the analysis has held up well, and the policy options discussed remain relevant. While the regulatory climate has changed, and while the gas shortage foreseen has become obvious, we have decided that the new information would not change the study sufficiently to justify further delay.

A number of persons have contributed to this study by reading earlier drafts of it and making meaningful and useful suggestions. We would like to express our special appreciation to Dr. Haskell P. Wald, Chief, Office of Economics, Federal Power Commission; Dr. Charles Stalon, Federal Power Commission and Southern Illinois University; and to our colleagues, Dr. Thomas Martinsek, Roger Christ, and George Conour of the Department of Economics, Southern Illinois University, Carbondale. The errors or misunderstandings remaining in this book are, of course, ours.

1

State Production Taxes and Federal Regulation

The major natural gas producing states each levy a severance tax on natural gas as it is produced. This severance tax brought a substantial $200 million in revenues to the states during 1967, and the figure has increased considerably since that time.[1] Severance taxes, because of the nature of the natural gas field market and the supply-demand relationship which now appears to exist (see chapter 3), are largely shifted onto consumers, and many of these consumers are residents of nonproducing states. The producing states, therefore, through the imposition of state natural resource severance taxes, have shifted a portion of their domestic tax burden upon the citizens of other states. The results of the analysis below indicate that an even more substantial portion could be shifted with appropriate state tax action.

The federal cost-based regulation of the field price of natural gas, as it is now administered, facilitates this tax shifting by allowing taxes paid to the producing states as charges recoverable through a higher regulated price at the wellhead. The states thus are encouraged (given generally accepted goal functions) to increase taxes which in turn raises the price of natural gas at the wellhead. At the same time, the federal natural gas regulatory agency, the Federal Power Commission (FPC), historically has considered its responsibility to be to maintain field prices at the lowest level consistent with appropriate natural gas supply and equitable treatment of the natural gas producers. If this analysis is correct, a conflict of interest thus exists between the producing states and the FPC.

---

[1] See Table 4, Appendix 2. Consistent data for the breakdown between interstate and intrastate sales for the period after 1967 are not available.

1

The focus of the conflict between these parties in the past has been within the context of the various natural gas producer cases, where the gas producing interests *within* a producing state provided the impetus for opposition to federal price control. When, as portions of this study indicate, higher severance taxes can benefit a broad spectrum of the producing state, this conflict may take on a new and even more serious dimension; the state may raise these taxes to take advantage of the situation created by regulation. It is on this potential, basic, intergovernmental conflict that this study is focused.

While the revenue motive of the states in imposing severance taxes is clear on the surface at least, the rationale behind federal regulation of the sale for resale of natural gas at the wellhead is not. Operationally, a sufficient reason for regulation of natural gas price at the wellhead is that it is the law.[2] For our purposes something more than a legalism is required, hence some consideration of the rationale behind gas price regulation is an appropriate part of this introduction, serving as background to an analysis of the specific problem dealt with in this book.

Market Imperfection
Rationale for Regulation

The traditional equity view of government regulation of public utilities, and of the field sales of natural gas, is that a ceiling price should be set equal to average cost in order to prevent unjust enrichment of the producer who uses his (presumed) monopoly power to restrict output and raise price. A further rationale based on the same analysis leads to the prescription of a regulated price equal to average cost in order to minimize the misallocation of resources inherent in a price above marginal cost (under the usual assumptions). In both rationales the policy result is the same—the private firm would receive a price just sufficient to meet its revenue requirements.

The application of this policy to the use of reproducible resources in elastic supply is both obvious and generally satisfactory because revenue requirements are equal to the current market value of the productive factors consumed. When, as in the natural gas industry, a significant portion of the revenue is required to cover production taxes and rental or quasi-rental charges, limited ultimately only by the demand characteristics in the final product market, a circular relationship between the observed revenue requirements to the firm and the price allowed under regulation is created. As will be demonstrated in chapter 3, under certain conditions this relationship offers an opportunity for the producing states to raise taxes on gas production and thereby transfer income from without to within the state.

---

[2]Natural Gas Act, 52 *Stat.* 821 (1938).

Beyond the matter of circularity mentioned above, the monopoly rationale also must be tested as to its factual applicability to the gas production industry. Voluminous study, the bulk of which has become familiar to most persons working in this field, has been devoted to this subject, but firm conclusions on the issue are not easy because of the institutional and technological complexities involved. Clearly, the industry does not fit the carefully drawn competitive model on either the demand or the supply side. While the classic competitive conditions do not by any means hold, in the absence of restrictions on the price interstate pipelines could bid for gas, the pragmatic test of availability of alternative gas supplies and of alternative sales outlets would be satisfied for most pipelines and most gas producers during most periods. Of course, because of random elements in both demand shifts and major reserve discoveries, long-term gas reserve contracts, immobility of pipelines, and long lead times to bring new reserves on the market, there are transitory periods of market power for virtually all producers and purchasers, and perhaps virtually permanent market power for a few. Such imperfections in the market most likely do not alter its basic configuration, and hence in this book the assumption is made that in the absence of producer price regulation the primary noncompetitive effect of the existing market structure comes in the form of transitory (but perhaps significant) market dislocation.

The existence of these dislocations has given rise to the market imperfections rationale for regulation, with a policy prescription of regulation to dampen major shifts in prices and to assure the industry that it will not be subjected to permanent price shifts due to transitory submarket conditions. The basic market structure premise in the discussion below is that in the absence of regulation there would be workable competition with periods of significant market power bringing localized or temporary price and quantity discontinuities.

Time Preference Rationale

The difference between the discounted present value of a non-reproducible resource like a gas reserve to society and to its private owners creates a second possible rationale for regulation of the natural gas production industry. There are a number of possible causes of a divergence between the social and the private value of a gas reserve, but before these can be explored the allocative role of severance taxes and of the charge for non-reproducible resources should be noted. The term *non-factor costs* will be used to indicate charges of this nature.[3]

---

[3]Analytically, severance taxes and charges for non-reproducible resources are similar in that they are costs to producers and do not represent reproducible factors. The term

Under U. S. law, subsurface mineral rights are the severable property of the owner of the surface of the land, who may exact a payment for the right to remove those minerals. The payment required usually is levied in two institutionally derived parts, the first a payment for the right to sever minerals from the land and the second a portion of the value of the minerals actually severed. Analytically, the payment required is a form of Ricardian rent; its size is determined by the payment just sufficient to induce the mineral rights owner to allow exploitation by one potential exploiter rather than another. In the absence of taxes or other governmental action, the rent thus reflects the private market estimation of the discounted future value of different deposits of natural gas and determines the rate of reserve exploitation.

Should the socially optimal rate of resource exploitation be judged to diverge from the observed rate, some governmental action to equalize them may become justifiable in the total welfare sense. If the discounted present social value of future use of the resource is judged to be higher than its current price, the implication is that the exploitation rate has been too fast; if it is judged to be less than the current price, the implication is that the rate has been too low. In either event, neglecting decision and transaction costs, welfare could be raised by government action, in the first instance decreasing and in the second instance increasing the rate of resource consumption.

Implicit in much of the discussion surrounding natural gas regulation has been the view that, on balance, the rate of exploitation under free market conditions would be too rapid. The arguments used to support this position include assertions that the capital market is inadequate to present a viable waiting alternative to the private holder, that the social time preference is lower than that of the private sector, that some gas reserves are sold at variable rather than full costs because they are produced jointly with oil, and, perhaps most telling, that the segmented ownership of a common pool of natural gas at best forces all owners to act on the highest discount rate among the individual owners, and at worst leads to competitive exploitation. The important counterassertion to these arguments is that the future value of natural gas reserves is overestimated because of the potential functional

---

non-factor costs, therefore, will refer to those elements included in the price of natural gas which are not costs of reproducible factors of production. Royalties and lease bonuses paid to landowners would be characterized in this usage as non-factor costs. The individual mineral rights owners have no alternative use for the gas reserve, and hence any positive price which was certain over time would be sufficient to keep the reserves committed to the gas industry. Production taxes paid to the states are included as producer costs in area ceiling price determinations by the FPC, yet these taxes represent the performance of no economic function. They also are included here under non-factor costs. Occasionally the term *rental elements* is used synonomously with non-factor costs.

replacement or supplementation of domestic natural gas by alternative resources such as atomic power, liquid natural gas importation, and coal conversion. Whichever position is taken with regard to the issue of rate of exploitation, it is clear that federal regulatory activities—and certainly state severance taxes—have affected that rate. The issue of intertemporal allocation of the natural gas resource base thus has underlain much of the discussion which ostensibly has dealt with other matters altogether.

Plan of Study

An examination of some of the background to the current field market regulation (see above), along with an explanation of the method by which the regulated price is determined (see chapter 2), is important to an understanding of some of the implications of this study. A field market model (chapter 3) then is developed which allows the analyst to examine the interaction of the interstate and the intrastate markets within the regulated context. Given this model, it then is possible to pose state goals and to analyze the nature of the severance tax which leads to the achievement of the goal chosen (chapter 4). Using some ranges of estimates for unobtainable values and 1967 data where available and appropriate, we calculate illustrative maximizing state taxes given the chosen goals (chapter 5). As presented, these approximations demonstrate that pursuit of a maximizing strategy by Texas and Louisiana would alter very significantly interstate income transfers, price levels, and interstate-intrastate natural gas allocation. In the main body of the analysis the restrictive assumption is made that the individual producing state serves a unique market, that is, there is assumed to be a one-to-one relationship between producing states and states which consume gas but do not produce it. This unrealistic assumption is relaxed partly in chapter 6 where the interaction in a common interstate market between two producing states with reference to severance tax policy is considered. Finally, in chapter 7, conclusions are drawn from the implications of this analysis for producer regulation, state taxing policy, intergovernmental relations, and interstate income transfers.

2

The Natural Gas Industry and Federal Regulation

The major developed natural gas reserves are found in the five southwestern states; gas from these reserves is transported by pipeline companies through high pressure pipelines to major consuming regions throughout the United States and to Canada.[1] The technology of the industry, which requires long-lived, capital-intensive transmission facilities, city distribution systems, and customer-owned ultimate use devices, together with the geographic inflexibility of reserve locations, lead distribution companies and pipelines to bargain with their respective suppliers for long-term supply contracts. These contracts provide some assurance that the firms will have sufficient use of the facilities to amortize the large capital investment required.

Local gas distribution firms were subjected early to local and state regulation as public utilities, but neither the localities nor the states could protect consumers from monopolistically exploitative charges from interstate gas pipeline firms.[2] The regulatory gap opened by interstate gas transmission was closed with FPC regulation of interstate pipelines under the 1938 Natural Gas Act.[3] In the 1954 *Phillips* case the Supreme Court declared that the Natural Gas Act applied to the sale of gas for resale in interstate commerce at

---

[1] See Table 1, Appendix 2.

[2] For a superb discussion of the structure of the early natural gas industry see Edward W. Kitch, "Regulation of the Field Market for Natural Gas by the Federal Power Commission," *Journal of Law and Economics* 11 (October 1968): 243-80.

[3] Natural Gas Act, 52 *Stat.* 821 (1938).

6

the wellhead, and in this fashion the FPC was given authority over the price of the commodity gas, as well as over the service of its interstate transportation.[4] The field price of gas which is sold for use within the producing state, or which is sold not for resale in interstate commerce, is not subject to control by the FPC, which raises some interesting analytical questions considered in the field market model (chapter 3).

The regulation of the field sales price by the FPC, after a series of false starts and much litigation, has been established under the area price method.[5] Briefly stated, this method treats the entire natural gas industry within a given geographic area as the regulated unit and seeks to provide the industry thus circumscribed with a price equal to the average cost of producing natural gas, including a return on industry investment. Individual companies are allowed to make contracts with any available buyers at any price at or below the regulated price for the area. Except for the inability to abandon a sales contract without permission, the necessity to file certain information, the requirement of a certificate of convenience and necessity, and some uncertainty as to the inviolability of the established ceiling (contract) price, the individual producing firm has an incentive structure similar to the opportunities and constraints of a firm facing a market-determined price.

The costs which are used as the basis for the regulated ceiling price are determined by examining both industry and aggregated company data, with some of the cost factors calculated on an area and others on a national basis. The rate of return on capital is selected, in part, by reference to return in other industries. A distinction is made between gas reserves of which the finding, developing, and producing conceptually were and were not influenced by federal regulation of field price. Those gas reserves conceptually not influenced by regulation are costed on a historical basis by areas. The goal is a price which, for the group as a whole, returns historically expended costs plus a reasonable return on capital. For gas which conceptually was searched for, developed, and produced after the inception of regulation, the price level sought is one associated with current revenue requirements so that the producer will have an incentive to replace gas reserves expended. Hence, the desired price is one just sufficient to retain in the industry enough productive factors to maintain the level of gas supply sought.[6] Thus, it is primarily this last, the "new" gas price, which is of significance to resource allocation.

---

[4]*Phillips Petroleum Co.* v. *Wisconsin,* 347 U.S. 672 (1954).

[5]Area Rate Proceeding AR 61-1 (Permian Basin) *Opinion No. 468,* 34 FPC 159; *Permian Basin Rate Cases,* 390 U.S. 747 (1968).

[6]Throughout this paper the supply of natural gas will be described by a function relating price to the optimal annual production of natural gas from natural gas reserves

FPC Ceiling Price Determination

The estimation of the factor cost element of the expenditures in bringing natural gas to the pipeline is beset by difficulties, not the least of which is the analytical impossibility of allocating costs to a joint product. Natural gas often is produced with liquid petroleum, and the allocation of costs between these two physical products from a given well is strictly arbitrary. Even in the case of a field which produces only natural gas, some portion of the exploration cost must be assigned to liquid petroleum because of the nonzero probability that, *ex ante,* exploration was undertaken that could have led to petroleum production. The arbitrariness of the allocations required has been smothered in complex costing formulas which have been condoned legally because they are not obviously unreasonable, but no economic comfort should be taken from this fact.[7]

Under the area price method, the estimation of the non-factor costs is of particular interest to the economist because of the policy implications of the manner in which non-factor costs are reflected in the regulated price. Two of these costs are analytically similar to Ricardian rent, and the third, severance taxes, has some social rent overtones. The bonus payment portion of non-factor costs is one element in the regulatory category termed gas lease acquisition costs. It reflects, in part, the differential value of a prospective gas reserve as compared to the marginal reserve. The other form which return to owners of mineral rights takes is royalty, a portion of the value of produced mineral reserves. Royalty variations among pricing regions suggest the differential value of gas in different locations and the level of risk associated with the opportunity of finding gas of a given quality. A minimum royalty of 12.5 percent has been institutionalized in the petroleum industry. This level forms the base from which there is an upward adjustment determined by the negotiated expected differential value of the land area in question as compared to the marginal (12.5 percent royalty) prospects. While one might expect the level of royalty to vary from some positive value approaching zero for the marginal prospects to a high level for high value, virtually risk-free

---

that would exist at that price. This definition accepts changes in the rate of exploitation from a given reserve size due to changes in the price, interest rate, and so forth, to the extent that such variability is technically, institutionally, and legally permissible. Implicitly, the demand for natural gas reserves for dedication to given uses represents a derived demand for those reserves from a direct demand for an annual flow of gas. Since the analysis herein deals with the effects of various factors on the long-run supply and demand for gas, the effects of such matters as the current stock of reserves on gas prices and availability in the short run can be ignored.

[7]Clark A. Hawkins, *The Field Price Regulation of Natural Gas* (Tallahassee, Florida: Florida State University Press, 1969), presents a very cogent analysis of the cost allocation problem in natural gas producer regulation.

reserves, the observed limits of royalty percentages are considerably narrower. Various subsidiary conditions exist between the gas producer and the mineral rights owner which in fact alter the value of the contract, so some recognition of differential reserve value is sometimes given beyond the differences in the level of the bonus payment and royalty rate.[8]

The final non-factor cost element in the regulated ceiling price is the one on which this study is focused, namely, the severance tax imposed by the producing state on each unit of gas produced. The FPC concluded in its deliberations leading to *Permian* that actual taxes paid were to be covered by the ceiling price because such taxes were a revenue requirement for the producers. Hence, a change in taxes would be reflected directly in the allowed regulated price and, should the gas purchase contract permit, would be shifted directly and immediately upon the purchaser of the gas in the field. Given the cost-based regulation of the transactions between the wellhead and the burner tip, under ordinary assumptions the severance tax would be incident upon the ultimate consumer.

One complexity of some relevance to the determination of the regulated ceiling price for natural gas is the liquid lease credit; explanation of it provides an appropriate vehicle for elaboration of the overall process of ceiling price determination. The regulated price is adjusted by the per-gas-unit revenue from the sale of liquid petroleum products which accrues to the producer, with production taxes and royalties netted out before the credit is applied. In Texas and Louisiana, the two major gas producing states, a different production tax is applied to these liquid condensates than is applied to the processed natural gas itself.[9] Hence, while these credits must be included in the original area rate determination calculations, the effects of these credits upon state tax revenue from the natural gas production tax are independent of any changes in this tax, although these credits do affect the price which ultimate consumers must pay.

After the values for the factor and non-factor costs are determined, the regulated area price may be easily calculated, as the example below indicates. Once we establish the following,

$$P_r: \qquad \text{regulated area price (ceiling)}$$

---

[8]See Table 2, Appendix 2, for the estimated royalty rates in the major southwestern producing states.

[9]*Presiding Examiner's Initial Decision on Texas Gulf Coast Area Rates,* Docket No. AR 64-2 (16 September 1968), pp. 78, 156; *Opinion No. 546, Opinion and Order Determining Just and Reasonable Rates for Natural Gas Producers in the Southern Louisiana Area,* Docket No. AR 61-2, p. 32.

C':   total factor costs (In FPC procedure these include lease acquisition costs, a portion of which are lease bonus payments, a non-factor cost.)

r: royalty (percent), $0 \leqslant r < 1$

t: ad valorem production tax on gas, $0 \leqslant t < 1$

t':   ad valorem production tax on liquid condensates, $0 \leqslant t' < 1$

L':   gross liquid credit

L: net liquid credit,

then,

$$P_r = \frac{C' - L'(1-r)(1-t')}{(1-r)(1-t)} \quad .$$

Letting

$$C = \frac{C' - L'(1-r)(1-t')}{(1-r)} \quad ,$$

$$P_r = \frac{C}{(1-t)} \quad .$$

This will give P_r when considering only changes in the production tax. As an example, assume the following values:[10]

$C' = 16.86¢/\text{Mcf}$

$L' = 4.61¢/\text{Mcf}^{11}$

$r = 14$ percent

$t = 7$ percent

[10]William T. Loring, *Current, National, Average Unit Cost of Finding, Developing and Producing Reserves of Gas-Well Gas for the Total United States Gas Producing Industry,* Docket No. AR 67-1 (Other Southwest Area), Schedule No. 1, Sheet 1 of 2.

[11]Obtained from the net liquid credit in *supra.*

$t' = 7$ percent[12]

$$P_r = \frac{16.86 - 4.61 \ (1 - 0.14)(1 - 0.07)}{(1 - 0.14)(1 - 0.07)}$$

$$= \frac{16.86}{0.80} - 4.61 = 21.08 - 4.61$$

$$= 16.47¢/\text{Mcf}.$$

The calculated unit revenue requirement of the producer of natural gas would thus be 16.47¢/Mcf, given our assumed values.

The "Price" of
Natural Gas at the Wellhead

The "price" of natural gas at the wellhead perhaps is conceptually clear, but is operationally difficult to observe. First, natural gas as it is produced is not homogeneous, with such characteristics as heat value, purity, pressure, deliverability, and field volume affecting its value to the purchaser. Contractual arrangements surrounding gas transfer also affect its value, the most important perhaps being the rate at which the reservoir is to be depleted, with the producer, within broad limits, seeking a higher rate in order to realize a faster return of his capital. The length of the contract, possible renegotiation of price, future sharing of tax liability, and the nature of penalties for non-performance all enter into the price negotiations. The final major factor affecting the value of natural gas is transportation costs. Distance from consuming markets is one major determinant of these costs and level of production within the region is another. The distance effect is obvious; the volume effect is understandable once the large economies of scale in pipeline transport are considered.

For the above and other reasons then, the value of a unit of raw gas from different deposits is not identical to the prospective purchaser, and the contractual terms surrounding a sale alter its true price, which explains some of the difficulties in applying the field market model discussed below. The FPC, in its regulation, costs out the value of some of the most significant contract and raw gas variables and requires that the ceiling price be adjusted accordingly. While these adjustments are helpful to the analyst, it remains impossible to be definitive about field price comparisons among gas sales contracts and for different time periods. For these same reasons, the regulated price is not easy to relate explicitly to some market clearing or equilibrium rate, even were that rate determinable. The market itself does not give easily observable or unambiguous information.

---

[12] Although, as noted previously, t and t' are sometimes different, the 7 percent value for both was used by Loring in the testimony referred to above.

Whatever the ceiling price means in market terms, and whether it is intended to reflect, on the one hand, a functionally competitive equilibrium price aside from monopoly or market imperfections, or, on the other hand, some socially efficient allocation of resources, it will affect the quantities of gas supplied and demanded differently, depending upon its relationship with the "equilibrium" price. Even with the above strictures about the inconclusiveness of the results of such comparisons, we still can analyze these relationships and then refer to market experience for an indication of which posited hypothesis best fits the observed behavior of the industry. Unfortunately, direct evidence to this end does not exist. All of the apparently plausible direct tests, such as a comparison of ceiling price to non-regulated prices, a direct observation of unsatisfied demand or excess supply, and the existence of an apparent black market, somehow are flawed. Even such secondary evidence as might be called forward is only suggestive. For example, one might expect divergence between the regulated and the equilibrium price to bring changes in the length of the queue in the field market and delays in service availability, but these indicators too are contaminated by FPC certification regulation. A few indications of market relationships are present, however, and are considered below.

The Relationship between Ceiling and Equilibrium Prices

It is convenient at this point to assert, leaving demonstration to a later point, that FPC ceiling price regulation of interstate jurisdictional sales can be interpreted as effective in economic terms over the entire industry, including that which is non-regulated. There thus is no distinction made in this section between the regulated and unregulated portions of the market.

Figure 1 is a schematic presentation of the industry with the ceiling price above the equilibrium price. A ceiling price at this level would have no direct effect on quantities supplied and demanded because the market price would only reach, but not exceed, the equilibrium level. Observed, workably competitive market conditions consistent with the hypothesis that the existing ceiling price was above the equilibrium price would include new contracts being filed substantially below the ceiling, stabilization or rationalization of the reserves-to-production ratio, little producing industry concern with the regulated price, and some variability of the gas sales price about the equilibrium. This variability (discussed briefly above) would occur as individual pipelines and producers reached agreements on particular contracts. Prices would vary because the needs of pipelines for new supplies cannot be smoothly articulated with their purchase of gas. Gas reserves usually are purchased by pipelines in large blocks, the full use of which would not occur until a growing market developed or until old reservoirs were more nearly depleted. Moreover, the random occurrence of reserve discoveries in any given local market also would alter the relative strengths of the parties at various times. Hence, depending on pipeline needs and reserve availability, some localized variability in reserve price could be expected.[13]

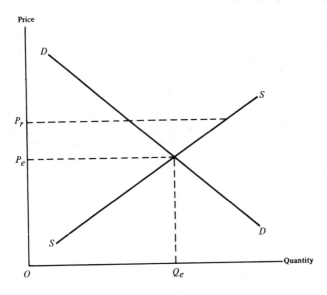

FIGURE 1

Figure 2 shows a ceiling price at the equilibrium price. At this level the ceiling price would be consistent with the long-run equilibrium price, with quantities supplied determined by costs of production (including the payment for current rather than future exploitation) and quantities demanded determined by the value of the gas to potential consumers. In the absence of shifts in costs of holding reserves, and so forth, the reserves-to-production ratio would be stabilized dynamically as the industry adjusted itself to the optimal levels of reserves needed to support a given quantity of sales.[14] Contract prices, taking into account the total package of conditions surrounding a sale, would be reasonably stable, and the particular price divergence from the equilibrium price brought on by temporary conditions would be dampened, at least on the upside. No long-run shortages or

---

[13]A good analysis of the factors affecting the relative bargaining strengths of pipelines and gas producers can be found in Paul W. MacAvoy, *Price Formation in the Natural Gas Fields: A Study of Competition, Monopsony and Regulation* (New Haven, Conn.: Yale University Press, 1962).

[14]The reserves-to-production (R/P) ratio as an optimal gas supply indicator has been much misused in the past. It has declined historically because of the reversal of the

surpluses of gas (ignoring random or fortuitous exploration results) would be evident; all potential purchasers could receive gas at the going price with a necessary lead time limited to that consistent with technological factors and costs subject only to failures of planning.

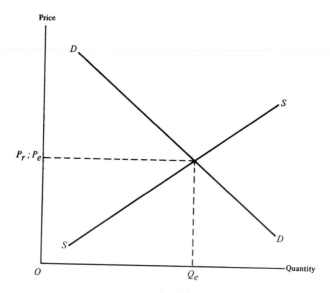

FIGURE 2

Figure 3 is drawn to demonstrate a relationship between the supply-demand functions and the regulated price such that a regulated price restricts the amount of gas offered for sale. In effect, buyers of natural gas are shown as being willing to purchase unavailable production at an established legal price. The quantity of gas actually sold is thus determined by interaction between the regulated price and the supply function, not by the interaction between demand and supply. From the diagram, the producers of natural gas,

---

excessively high R/P relationship that was established when natural gas, discovered accidentally during the process of drilling for oil, did not have a significant long-distance consuming market because of the expense of transportation. The decline to some extent thus merely reflected a move toward an optimal stock of gas to service the production needs.

Gas can be produced from a reservoir at somewhat different rates, within limits, and therefore different R/P ratios could be optimal depending on the relative costs of the factors used in rapid, as contrasted to slow, depletion. The lower limit of the permissible R/P ratio depends upon deliverability from the reservoirs, and deliverability falls as a given reservoir nears depletion. Because the prices of the factors in the gas production function vary, no one optimal ratio can be defined over time. See Milton Russell, "The Adequacy of Natural Gas Reserves," *Public Utilities Fortnightly,* 14 October 1965, pp. 70-81.

at the regulated price, will not make more than Q_r gas available even though at that same price purchasers in the field would be willing to purchase more. Should the regulated price be raised to P_e, however, the market would be cleared and no unsatisfied demand would result. Thus, the ceiling price set by the FPC is shown as having a constraining effect (the market clearing quantity would be higher in its absence) and a permanent gas shortage, as measured by a private market equilibrium, exists.

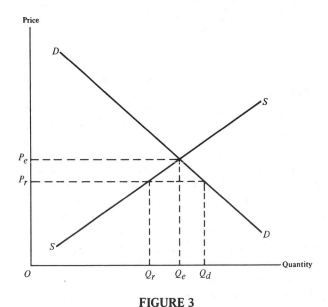

FIGURE 3

The limited amount of gas available is rationed among the prospective purchasers by FPC certification delays, by non-price direct rationing (such as FPC "inferior use" certification denials), by pipeline refusal to seek additional service areas, and, ultimately, by the cost to prospective purchasers of the delay in obtaining gas. This latter cost plays the equilibratory role as it raises the total price of gas (including both monetary cost and the waiting element) to a level which restricts the quantity demanded to the quantity supplied. In other words, with a regulated price below the equilibrium price, the length of the queue at the consuming and, hence, the pipeline levels must be sufficiently long (costly) to force enough potential consumers to reduce fuel use or to substitute other fuels for gas to bring quantity demanded into equilibrium with the (restricted) amount supplied. This equilibrium does not imply satisfaction; the prospective parties to gas sales contracts perceive that both prospective buyers and sellers would be better off with the attainable higher price *and* higher level of gas sales.

Observed facts consistent with the hypothesis that the ceiling price is below the equilibrium (Figure 3) would include the following: (1) the majority of the contracts were being negotiated at, not below, the ceiling price; (2) R/P ratios were going through a period of decline (at least until a new equilibrium ratio was reached); (3) a queue of potential purchasers of gas existed, the length of which, while first growing, eventually would tend to stabilize; (4) direct efforts were being undertaken by both purchasers and sellers of gas to avoid the ceiling price; and (5) support for higher wellhead prices was being granted by prospective purchasers of gas.

Observed Ceiling-
Equilibrium Price Relationship

The natural gas field market over the recent past (1967 to early 1970) has exhibited a number of conditions consistent with the hypothesis that the regulated price has fallen below the market clearing price and inconsistent with the alternative hypotheses that the ceiling price has remained above or equal to the equilibrium price.[15] Observations on the ceiling-equilibrium price relationship during this time are particularly interesting because the period appears to have been one of transition. A first, and very rough, indication of this situation is the observed experience with natural gas production and reserves. Natural gas consumption has continued to increase (in 1969 at a 7 percent rate). At the same time, the proven reserves from which this gas can be drawn dropped in 1969 for the second year in a row, the first drops noted since 1946 when reserves first were estimated by the American Gas Association (AGA).[16]

This drop in reserves was the joint result of an unprecedented and unexpected continued increase in natural gas consumption and of the decline in new reserves found. While discovery of new gas reserves is in part stochastic, the level of investment in gas exploration, given lags, determines within broad limits the quantity of gas found. The observed results for 1969

---

[15] Some industry analysts jump to the unwarranted conclusion that a finding that the ceiling price is below the equilibrium price in the private market is a sufficient reason to raise the ceiling price. No such policy conclusion follows because the goals of regulation are broader, or at least may be broader, than merely establishing a more stable market equilibrium. Income redistribution (both among individuals and regions), nonmarket resource allocation, alterations of economic power balances, and rectification of a divergence between social and private optimal rates of exploitation all may be a part of the total goal function of regulation. Whatever the goal function, however, the relationship between the ceiling price and a market-clearing price is important, if for no other reason than that in our economy the burden of proof for the desirability of such market interference would lie on those who sought it.

[16] From figures contained in "Gas reserves skid again only more so," *Oil and Gas Journal,* 6 April 1970, p. 61.

and the previous five years are consistent with a situation where the price is less than necessary to induce producers to extend their resource commitments to maintain previous R/P ratios. The ratio in 1968 dropped to 14.8 from the previous year's 15.8 level, and in 1969 dropped further to 13.3.[17] The continued increase in consumption has been supported by a rapid drawdown in reserves which cannot continue. In effect, the sub-equilibrium price has shown itself in a deterioration of the reserve backing for current gas deliveries. On the basis of short term experience then (and keeping in mind the inaccuracies and possible distortions of the measurements involved), the results of the past year with reference to reserves appear to be consistent with the hypothesis that the regulated natural gas price is below the market equilibrium price.

The second source of information with regard to the relative level of regulated price is the observed behavior of the purchasers of natural gas in the field and, in turn, of their proximate customers, the natural gas distributors. The Independent Natural Gas Association of America (INGAA), a major trade group, moved to intervene in the Southern Louisiana area rate case after the FPC decision of 25 September 1968. INGAA called for further argument on the supply situation in a motion before the commission described as "pleading with the commission for rates to permit expansion of gas supply–'the life blood of the pipeline companies.' "[18]

Purchasers of gas in the field have reacted to the level of the regulated price by bidding for gas through non-price concessions to the producers in the classic gray market fashion, although it is difficult to determine whether the concessions are due to the general restraint on price or to the specific prices set as related to given reservoirs. For whichever reason, contract provisions have been adopted to provide a more profitable package to the producers.

The natural gas distributors as a group have reversed their historic and strongly held position that natural gas prices should be vigorously restrained at the wellhead and that the supply situation was in no way serious. In December 1968 the AGA, in a formal letter to the FPC, cited falling exploration and reduced levels of new reserves as a matter of considerable concern to its members, and suggested that the FPC, "because of the imminence of a critical gas-supply-availability situation," reexamine producer prices. "The necessary drilling to avoid an impending shortage," AGA said, "awaits only this commission's acknowledgement that additional economic

---

[17] Ibid.

[18] Gene T. Kinney, "Unity reached in drive for higher wellhead price," *Oil and Gas Journal,* 23 December 1968, p. 16.

incentive is needed . . . . Distributor utilities now seeking to contract for long-term supplies from interstate pipelines are being refused."[19]

In this December 1968 letter the distributors noted that it was likely they soon would be unable to cover all of their growing gas requirements and that there was a high probability the consuming public would suffer from future restrictions on the availability of gas at the city gate. The AGA stated that the commission should take a new look at its methods of establishing natural gas prices in order to insure sufficient incentives to producers, pointing to settlements negotiated among the industry components as a possible vehicle. Finally, the AGA noted the importance to Eastern consumers of the potential gas supplies from off-shore Louisiana and suggested that methods be established to speed the construction of new pipelines into that area.[20] At the time of this communication some question was raised as to whether this position represented a distributor consensus. No substantial evidence has been made public tending to discredit the position as reflecting that of the AGA membership, and some further supporting distributor actions followed.[21]

In summary, during the recent past gas pipelines and distributors both have indicated their concern about the availability of natural gas and implicitly have affirmed their willingness to accept the risk of not being able to pass on higher commodity costs because of demand characteristics in the consuming markets.

The third factor consistent with the hypothesis that the equilibrium price is above the current regulated price, at least in some gas markets, has been the willingness of many of the parties, including consumer interest representatives, to agree to contractual terms at rates higher than the ceiling price. While it usually has been impossible to achieve unanimity on supra-ceiling negotiated settlements, proposals have come forward apparently with a high likelihood of success.[22]

The wide concern about natural gas supplies has evoked a response from the Federal Power Commission and from some of its commissioners. The FPC established a proceeding to investigate off-shore gas supply and cost conditions in southern Louisiana on 20 March 1969, in part to determine the

---

[19] Ibid., p. 15. Prior to the time of this letter, distributor members of the AGA had been very active in area rate cases; they sponsored testimony and argued in briefs that no supply problem existed and that a price covering observed revenue requirements would provide sufficient incentive for natural gas exploration.

[20] Ibid., pp. 15, 16.

[21] "Campaign for higher gas price builds," *Oil and Gas Journal,* 10 February 1969, p. 38.

[22] "Negotiated area rate may not be dead," *Oil and Gas Journal,* 14 April 1969, p. 89.

effectiveness of the established ceiling in bringing forth adequate supplies. The opening of this proceeding at the very time that the basic Southern Louisiana opinion was affirmed is consistent with misgivings about gas supply and pricing procedures expressed in statements issued by many of the FPC commissioners, although it should be clearly realized that a speech by a commissioner does not represent either settled policy or a vote on a substantive issue.[23]

One final point should be made in this discussion of the position of ceiling and equilibrium prices. The producers have resisted the actual prices established as well as the concept of regulation itself, and by this action have lent some credence to the hypothesis that the ceilings are restrictive. The long hearings undergone, the willingness of individual producers to engage in expensive litigation to appeal the general price levels set, and the actions firms have taken in seeking to avoid the restrictions of regulation all provide circumstantial evidence that the regulatory prices formulated have been thought by the producers to have been binding on them. While there is ample reason to doubt the public pronouncements of the regulated firms, the nature of their actions in seeking to avoid the particular price restraints which have been established testifies in some degree to the effectiveness of the restraint. It would appear that producing firms have gone far beyond the ceremonial posture.

In summary, the hypothesis that the ceiling price for gas has been lower than the equilibrium price (in the industry as a whole, not making a judgment as to particular prices in particular areas) is certainly consistent with the observed data for the last few years. Whatever the situation earlier, no reasonable doubt now exists that the FPC's regulation during this period has indeed had the effect of a ceiling price. The wisdom of this restriction is beyond this analysis as is the cause for the development of effective restraint over the past few years. The wisdom of the restriction partly rests on estimates of the competitiveness of the field market and partly upon a judgment of how effectively the market mechanism, given existing institutions, reflects properly the social cost of current gas consumption. As to the second issue, the development of effective constraint over the past few years, the unexpectedly high growth in gas demand, tight capital markets, soft petroleum demand, negative investment effects from the existence of regulation, uncertainty both as to taxes and to regulation, and perhaps fortuitous results in exploration all have played a part. It is our task to develop a field market model and apply it to these existing conditions, especially as they relate to state severance taxes.

---

[23]Federal Power Commission, Docket Nos. AR 61-2 and AR 69-1, *Southern Louisiana Area Rate Proceeding, Opinion 546-A* (20 March 1969). The original Southern Louisiana decision was Federal Power Commission Docket No. AR 61-2, *Southern Louisiana Area Rate Proceeding, Opinion 546* (28 September 1968).

3

The Field Market Model

The field market model presented below facilitates an investigation of the effect of state severance tax rate variations on such factors as interstate income transfer, relative interstate-intrastate gas consumption, the quantities of natural gas supplied and demanded, producing industry revenue, and producing state tax revenue. In the next chapter this model is utilized to examine the interaction of the federal regulatory pattern with different state severance tax levels. In this manner optimizing behavior by the producing states and by gas regulating authorities can be posited, given assumptions as to goals and existing conditions.

The basic formulation of the model used in this book is in terms of the individual gas producing state in the long run. However, if the supply and demand functions referred to are interpreted as the aggregate functions for the entire U. S. natural gas industry, the general or qualitative conclusions reached are applicable to the national industry as a whole. The policy implications of this model remain sound at this higher level of generalization. A somewhat separate problem is encountered when a two-state, interactive model is considered, and this matter is taken up in chapter 6.

Figure 4 represents a market for natural gas within a state, given the workable competition assumption discussed on pages 2-3. The supply function is depicted by line S. It is intended to suggest the long-run relationship between price received by producers and total annual amount produced at each price (see footnote 6, chapter 2). The producer, the decision-making unit, makes no distinction between his factor and non-factor costs—both are charges against his revenues. Hence, this supply function contains an allowance for both severance taxes and rent. AM and BR are individual demand curves which represent the intrastate and interstate demand for natural gas and in general will be different. No conclusions from this analysis depend upon the shape or position of the functions as drawn in Figure 4. *BGU* is the combined or total demand curve, including both intrastate and interstate demand. These demand functions indicate the annual amounts that would be purchased if a particular price, once established, continued to exist. If there were no restrictions on the interstate price, the market-clearing price P_e would hold in both the intrastate and interstate markets, with Q_e the total amount demanded and supplied. A shift in any one of these functions would establish a new, long-run equilibrium price and quantity to which the industry would adjust over time. If *AM* were the demand curve associated with the intrastate market, *OL* would be sold intrastate, *ON* interstate.

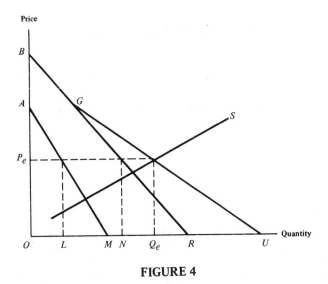

FIGURE 4

If we now add the condition that the interstate price is subject to federal regulation and assume that the regulated price, P_r, is below P_e, we would have the situation shown in Figure 5. The mutual relationship of P_r and P_e is of central importance in the following analysis, as are the methods by which each is determined. P_r is assumed to be established by the FPC in the manner described on pages 8-11. P_e always will refer to the long-run market-clearing price which would be established competitively in the absence of an effective ceiling price. In Figure 5, P_e is determined simultaneously by the intersection of the supply function and the combined demand function, *BGU*. If, as we will posit in the application of this model to the issues in question, the supply function shifts due to a change in the production tax, P_e will change accordingly. Whether or not P_r alters with a change in the production tax is determined by the FPC in the manner described previously, being part of the institutional framework within which the model operates.

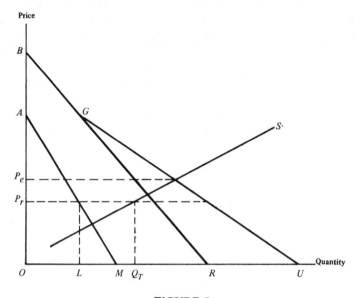

FIGURE 5

All of the major producing states we are considering sell gas in both the intrastate and interstate markets, and marginal gas sellers dedicating new reserves are free to sell in either market as they choose. An essentially free and competitive market exists. We posit, then, that if P_r is less than P_e, over time virtually the same price, P_r, will exist for all of the customers of a given state, subject to slight price differences associated with the ascertainable seller costs generated by selling in a regulated environment, and subject as well to a slight premium from intrastate consumers to overcome producer indifference. The mechanism for price convergence toward the regulated price (restricting the analysis to the situation where gas is sold in both markets) follows the usual pattern: if the unregulated intrastate price tended to be greater than P_r, producers would, over time, shift sales from the interstate into the higher-priced intrastate outlets. The resulting increase in quantity supplied would bring down the intrastate price. Conversely, no profit maximizing producers would sell into the intrastate market if interstate purchasers were offering a higher, though regulated, price (subject, of course, to the above-mentioned possible cost differences in selling interstate). Hence, although the intrastate price is not regulated it will tend toward identity with P_r, although in periods of market change the adjustment may not be instantaneous but may take observable periods of time. In line with our earlier discussion, *price* is defined as the total value of the package of conditions surrounding the sale and is not limited simply to the stated price in cents per thousand cubic feet ($\cent$/Mcf) of gas. Thus, in Figure 5 amount OQ_T will be supplied, with OL going to the intrastate market and the remaining amount, LQ_T, being sold interstate. Note particularly that whenever there is excess demand (due to P_r below P_e) the supply function, together with P_r, determines the total quantity sold.

The supply function itself, as has been noted, is shifted by changes in the level of severance taxes. Most of the major gas producing states, including Texas, have an ad valorem production tax on natural gas and this formulation is used in this analysis; a specific type tax such as that found in Louisiana requires a slightly different formulation but also could be accommodated. In establishing the definition of the supply function, taking explicit account of severance taxes, let the function in Figure 5 be:

$$P^o = A + BQ, \qquad B > 0, \tag{3.1}$$

where the superscript on P is meant to indicate that the production tax has a value of zero. If an ad valorem production tax t is now imposed (t between zero and one), in order for the original amount to be supplied, it would be necessary for the price to rise sufficiently so that after the tax is paid the supplier still would be left with P^o dollars, the original price for each unit. In symbols, with P denoting the price *inclusive* of the tax, this requires that

$$P^o = P - (P \times t) = P(1 - t). \tag{3.1a}$$

Substituting the right-hand expression of (3.1a) for P^o in (3.1) results in

$$P(1 - t) = A + BQ.$$

Dividing by $(1 - t)$, one obtains

$$P = (A + BQ)/(1 - t), \tag{3.2}$$

which is the supply function that will be used in the following analysis. From (3.2) it can be seen that as t increases the required price, inclusive of the production tax, necessary to bring forth some given quantity, Q, also must increase.

The field market model and the operative federal regulatory techniques now will be used to analyze the opportunity presented to producing states to achieve various goals by alterations in the severance tax rates imposed. This process requires postulation of alternative state goals and then determination of the necessary conditions for realization of those goals.

4

Tax Strategy to Fulfill Posited Goals

Severance tax rates are directly and completely within the control of the individual producing state. The tax rate chosen can be presumed, therefore, to be a fit instrument of public policy within that state. The purpose of this section is to consider alternative public policies which the state might wish to pursue and then to determine the necessary tax rate conditions under which each policy might be achieved. Clearly, policies most often are not designed to follow one goal alone; *the* goal is a compromise among a variety of possible alternatives. Nevertheless, it is useful for analytical purposes to isolate goals as objectives in order to show in clearer relief those compromises which ultimately might result. No effort is made here to identify and discuss all potential goals. Instead, the goals selected were chosen to represent somewhat reasonable attitudes which might be taken within a particular state should the policy-making body be responsive to what could be termed the welfare effects on the taxpayers and citizens. This matter is considered further in chapter 7.

Four goals suitable for analysis may be posited with reference to severance tax policies of the producing states. *Goal 1:* The state might seek that non-negative tax rate which would maximize intrastate consumption of natural gas on the grounds that the secondary economic development effects of such intrastate consumption are positive and are preferred to the alternatives. (The possibility exists, although we do not consider it, of negative taxes or of special state expenditures to achieve this goal.) *Goal 2:* The state might choose to maximize revenue from natural gas, defined as the sum of state tax revenues and revenues received by natural gas producers within the state. *Goal 3:* The state might choose to maximize state severance tax revenues. *Goal 4:* The state might choose to maximize state tax revenues from out-of-state consumers.

**Goal 1: Maximization
of Intrastate Consumption**

The policy goal of maximizing intrastate gas sales has surface appeal to those producing state observers who note that consumption of gas within the state leads to higher levels of output and employment associated with gas-using industries. If a policy invoking this latter-day form of mercantilist thought were followed, the producing state would sacrifice the revenue from out-of-state consumers which could be used to support even more productive enterprises than those maintained through retention of the gas within the state. Under the usual assumptions regarding the functioning of a market, the goal of maximizing intrastate sales thus would appear to reduce state welfare. Nevertheless, the attraction of this alternative to some decision makers remains. Starting with this goal of maximum intrastate consumption, our field market model, and a regulated price of gas below the equilibrium price, an analysis can be made of the optimal tax rate to fulfill this goal should it be chosen.

The initial conditions shown in Figure 6 are the same as those in Figure 5. The regulated price, P_r, is less than P_e, thus embodying the assumption that excess demand exists. At price P_r producers are willing to supply quantity OQ_T. Intrastate consumers, represented by demand function AM, are fully satisfied at this price, purchasing an amount represented by OL. A reduction in the production tax would shift the supply function in Figure 6 downward from S to S', as per equation (3.2). Furthermore, it has been established that

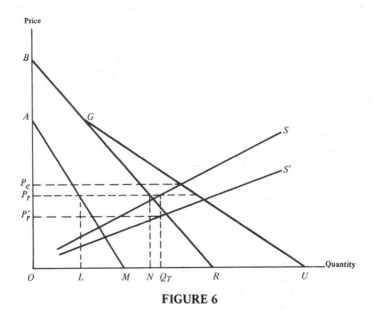

FIGURE 6

under the currently existing type of ceiling price regulation, the ceiling price also would be reduced. As shown before on p. 10 the ceiling price can be described as a function of the production tax, namely

$$P_r = C/(1 - t), \tag{4.1}$$

where C again represents all allowable costs of production other than the severance tax. As before, t can take on any value between zero and, but not including, one. Therefore, in Figure 6 the regulated price would be reduced to P_r'.

It is easy to prove, using equations (3.2) and (4.1), under the assumption of the existence of excess demand, that there will be no change in the quantity supplied. The existence of excess demand implies that P_r, in fact, will be an effective constraint on price, hence P of (3.2) will equal P_r of (4.1) and, therefore,

$$\frac{C}{1-t} = \frac{A + BQ}{1-t} . \tag{4.2}$$

Multiplying through by $(1 - t)$ and solving for Q,

$$Q = \frac{C - A}{B} . \tag{4.3}$$

From (4.3) it is obvious that the quantity supplied, Q, is constant, being independent of any changes in t as long as excess demand exists.

Thus, with the existence of excess demand and given present FPC policy with respect to production taxes, output does *not* depend upon the level of the production tax. As the tax is lowered, the prices in both markets (which are effectively identical due to the reasons discussed previously) fall. As can be seen in Figure 6, this results in additional gas being purchased in the intrastate market. Since the total amount of gas supplied does not change, less gas is left for the interstate market, which increases the amount of excess demand there. This process will continue as t is decreased toward zero. With zero tax intrastate gas consumption is at a maximum, insofar as it can be affected by a non-negative production tax.

Goal 2: Maximization of Total Revenue

A producing state may decide that state welfare could be increased by maximizing the total revenue from natural gas produced within the state. Such revenue, including both private and severance tax return, would be an indicator of the level of economic activity, a measure toward the increase of which politicians frequently are positive.

Total revenue from gas sales is merely the product of the price received and the quantity sold. In terms of Figure 7, total revenue, before a change in t, would be P_r times Q_T. It was proved in the previous case that the total quantity supplied will not vary with changes in the level of the production tax as long as the tax is non-negative and excess demand exists. Therefore, the supply function in Figure 7 can be shifted (by changes in t) all the way up to an intersection with BGU at f without reducing the quantity of gas sold. Since the price received, namely the regulated ceiling price, rises along with the tax [see equation (4.1)], then total revenue certainly increases with increases in t, under the present assumptions, until no excess demand exists. S' has been drawn in this special case by imposing a production tax of t', a value just sufficient to cause S' to intersect the combined demand curve BGU at point f. In other words, with a tax of t', P_r' equals P_e'; that is, the regulated ceiling price is the same as the market determined equilibrium price with the tax, and all excess demand is eliminated.

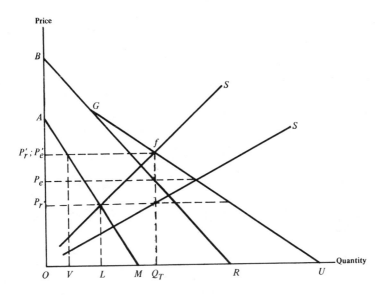

FIGURE 7

If t is increased beyond t', the total quantity of gas demanded and supplied will decrease, since P_e and Q_e are determined simultaneously by the demand and supply functions as the supply function moves upward or to the left beyond f. This simultaneous determination of P_e and Q_e would be the case for all values of t in the *absence* of ceiling price regulation. Start for the moment from such a condition without ceiling price controls. The tax rate could be found which would maximize total revenue, and the point at which the supply function intersects the demand function for this resulting t also would be determined. Reverting then to our ceiling price model, if this unconstrained revenue maximizing intersection point should lie to the right of point f, it would not be attainable under regulation and the optimal tax in this case would be t'. If, on the other hand, the unconstrained optimal tax shifted the supply function above or to the left of point f, then even under regulation the ascertained optimal t would be superior to t', and would result in a higher level of total industry revenue.

The process of determining the tax rate which will maximize total revenue from gas sales by an individual producing state may now be carried out through explicit formulation. It is first necessary to obtain an expression for the combined interstate and intrastate demand function since its intersection with the supply function determines P_e and Q_e. The product of P_e and Q_e is total revenue, the quantity to be maximized. As it is assumed in the following analysis that *some* gas always will be consumed in both the intrastate and the interstate markets, an expression only for line GU in Figure 7 is required. Any tax which would shift the supply function so that it intersected the combined demand function above point G, while amenable to the same analysis, is ignored to avoid unnecessary complication.

Given linear equations for the individual demand functions, it is a relatively simple matter to derive the equation for GU in terms of the parameters of the separate demand functions. If a_1 and a_2 are the intercepts, and b_1 and b_2 are the slopes, respectively, of the two demand functions, with a_1 less than a_2, the equation of interest, corresponding to the portion of the combined demand curve GU in Figure 7, is

$$P = a + bQ, \tag{4.4}$$

with P strictly less than a_1, thus insuring sales in both markets. In terms of the parameters of the individual demand functions (see Appendix 1 for proof), a is given by

$$a = \frac{a_1 b_2 + a_2 b_1}{b_1 + b_2}, \tag{4.5}$$

and b by

$$b = \frac{b_1 b_2}{b_1 + b_2}. \tag{4.6}$$

The procedure to be followed now merely involves solving equations (3.2) and (4.4) for the equilibrium values P_e and Q_e. The product of P_e and Q_e will be the total revenue to the industry, inclusive of taxes. Differentiating total revenue with respect to t then will give the change in total revenue with respect to an infinitesimally small incremental increase in t. Setting this derivative equal to zero will provide a necessary condition for the t which maximizes industry total revenue.[1] Recalling equation (3.2),

$$P = (A + BQ)/(1-t),$$

and solving (3.2) and (4.4) for P_e and Q_e,

$$Q_e = \frac{A - a(1-t)}{b(1-t) - B}; \quad \text{and} \tag{4.7}$$

$$P_e = a + b \left[\frac{A - a(1-t)}{b(1-t) - B} \right]. \tag{4.8}$$

Total (gross) revenue to the industry, price times quantity, is

$$TR = P_e \times Q_e . \tag{4.9}$$

The necessary condition for maximizing TR with respect to the tax rate, t, is

$$\frac{dTR}{dt} = P_e \frac{dQ_e}{dt} + Q_e \frac{dP_e}{dt} = 0. \tag{4.10}$$

dQ_e/dt may be obtained by differentiating equation (4.7):

$$\frac{dQ_e}{dt} = \frac{[b(1-t) - B] \, a + [A - a(1-t)] \, b}{[b(1-t) - B]^2}, \quad \text{or}$$

$$\frac{dQ_e}{dt} = \frac{a + bQ_e}{b(1-t) - B} .$$

Substituting from equation (4.4) for the numerator then yields

$$\frac{dQ_e}{dt} = \frac{P_e}{b(1-t)-B}, \quad 0 \leqslant t < 1. \tag{4.11}$$

Differentiating equation (4.4), with P_e and Q_e substituted for P and Q, gives

$$\frac{dP_e}{dt} = b \, \frac{dQ_e}{dt}, \tag{4.12}$$

---

[1]The general result that revenue is maximized at the point of unitary elasticity of the demand curve finds specific application in the formulation of Goal 2. We have chosen to derive rather than assert this result, however, because several of the expressions obtained in the process will be useful in determining the necessary conditions for optimal production taxes when pursuing Goals 3 and 4. Moreover, the process of derivation itself makes use of economic concepts which support the analysis below.

which, upon substitution of equation (4.11) for dQ_e/dt, becomes

$$\frac{dP_e}{dt} = \frac{bP_e}{b(1-t)-B}, \qquad 0 \leqslant t < 1. \tag{4.13}$$

Equations (4.11) and (4.13) now could be substituted into equation (4.10), giving the necessary condition for maximum gross revenue in terms of t, b, B, P_e, and Q_e. Instead of taking this step, an alternate, but equivalent (given linear functions), form will be obtained, expressing the necessary conditions in terms of the demand and supply elasticities, rather than in terms of the slopes b and B of these functions. This is done because economists usually are disposed to express statements about market supply and demand functions in terms of elasticities, finding them more convenient to interpret.

From equations (3.2) and (4.4) observe that the slopes of the demand and supply functions may be expressed as:

$$\frac{dP}{dQ_d} = b; \qquad \frac{dP}{dQ_s} = \frac{B}{(1-t)}.$$

If ϵ denotes the elasticity of supply, then

$$\epsilon = \frac{dQ_s}{dP}\frac{P}{Q_s}. \tag{4.14}$$

Since $\dfrac{dP}{dQ_s} = \dfrac{B}{(1-t)}$, then $\dfrac{dQ_s}{dP} = \left(\dfrac{1-t}{B}\right)$ because the supply function is assumed to be upward-sloping at all points and, therefore, is invertible. Substituting the latter expression into equation (4.14), with P_e and Q_e substituted for P and Q_s, yields

$$\epsilon = \frac{(1-t)}{B}\frac{P_e}{Q_e}. \tag{4.15}$$

Solving this for B, one obtains

$$B = \frac{(1-t)}{\epsilon}\frac{P_e}{Q_e}, \tag{4.16}$$

where B is the slope of the supply function with zero production tax, and ϵ is the elasticity of supply, given any non-negative level of t less than one. Similarly, the slope of the demand function, b, may be expressed as

$$b = \frac{1}{\eta}\frac{P_e}{Q_e}, \tag{4.17}$$

where η is the elasticity of the combined demand function.

It perhaps should be noted that the elasticities, η and ϵ, are not constants but actually are functions of t. As t varies, so does the market equilibrium position (P_e, Q_e). For any particular t, the symbol η refers to the elasticity of the market demand function evaluated at the resulting (P_e, Q_e) point. The same is true for ϵ.

Substituting equation (4.16) into (4.11) yields

$$\frac{dQ_e}{dt} = \frac{P_e}{\left[\frac{1}{\eta}\frac{P_e}{Q_e}(1-t) - \frac{(1-t)}{\epsilon}\frac{P_e}{Q_e}\right]} = \frac{Q_e}{\left(\frac{1}{\eta} - \frac{1}{\epsilon}\right)(1-t)}$$

$$= \frac{Q_e\eta\epsilon}{(\epsilon - \eta)(1-t)},$$

which becomes

$$\frac{dQ_e}{dt} = \frac{g\eta Q_e}{(1-t)}, \qquad g = \frac{\epsilon}{\epsilon - \eta} \quad > 0; 0 \leqslant t < 1. \tag{4.18}$$

Similarly, substituting (4.17) into (4.13) yields

$$\frac{dP_e}{dt} = \frac{gP_e}{(1-t)}, \qquad 0 \leqslant t < 1, \tag{4.19}$$

with g defined as in (4.18). Using these last two equations to rewrite (4.10),

$$\frac{dTR}{dt} = \frac{g\eta P_e Q_e}{(1-t)} + \frac{gP_e Q_e}{(1-t)} = 0,$$

or

$$\frac{dTR}{dt} = (\eta + 1)\frac{gP_e Q_e}{(1-t)} = 0, \tag{4.20}$$

giving a necessary condition for the optimal tax t in terms of the elasticities of supply (ϵ) and demand (η) and the equilibrium price and quantity, P_e and Q_e. Since the term $g\frac{P_e Q_e}{(1-t)}$ is strictly positive for positive values of t, P_e, and Q_e, equation (4.20) can be divided by this term, leaving $\eta + 1 = 0$, or $\eta = -1$. The necessary condition for maximum revenue to the industry, namely, that $dTR/dt = 0$, would be satisfied at the point where $\eta = -1$.

Thus, the optimal tax, if the state severance tax goal under regulation is to maximize total revenue to the industry inclusive of taxes, would be the rate which causes the supply function to intersect the demand function at the point of unitary elasticity of demand, if this critical point lies above point f in Figure 7. If the demand function exhibits unitary elasticity below point f, the optimal tax would be that which causes the supply function to intersect the demand function exactly at point f, eliminating excess demand. At point f the regulated ceiling price, P_r', becomes just equal to P_e', the price which the free market would establish *in the absence* of a constraining ceiling price. Starting with $P_r < P_e$, no reduction in quantity supplied will occur with an increase in tax whatever the elasticity of demand until excess demand is squeezed from the system by higher prices. Revenue thus continues to rise with increased taxes until that point is reached. Whatever the circumstance, then, to maximize total revenue (as defined) the producing state always would raise taxes sufficiently so that no unsatisfied demand existed. The optimal tax, however, could be even higher. Since unsatisfied demand has existed, a prima facie case exists that, given the posited goal, state severance taxes, at least since 1968, have been too *low* in the typical important gas producing state.

Goal 3: Maximization of Tax Revenue

The goal of maximizing production tax revenue from the natural gas industry may have considerable appeal to the governments of gas-producing states, especially if the quantities produced are large. In our analysis the ad valorem type tax is being considered because it is the most common. The amount of tax paid by the producer per unit of gas sold is obtained by multiplying the tax rate, t, times the selling price, P. Multiplying this product by the number of units sold, Q, then gives the total tax revenue. Under our assumptions, there will be only one price at which gas is exchanged. Therefore, if total revenue is denoted by T,

$$T = t \times P \times Q = t \times TR. \tag{4.21}$$

Referring to Figure 8, let S denote the supply function in the absence of a production tax of the type being considered. A tax sufficient to shift the supply function to, for example, S' would result in tax revenue equal to the cross-hatched area. Note that the producers' income has not changed with the imposition of the tax. As in the case of Goal 2, there will be no change in quantity supplied until the tax is raised sufficiently to eliminate the excess demand, that is, until the tax is raised sufficiently to shift S beyond S''. It is obvious that tax revenue will continue to increase until this point is reached, and to achieve the tax revenue maximization goal t will be *at least* such as to shift the supply function to the point where excess demand is eliminated.

To determine whether or not the supply function should be shifted above S'' in Figure 8, the same procedure should be followed as in Goal 2. Again, tax revenue, T, will be maximized with respect to the tax rate, t, ignoring any ceiling price constraint. The same test as in Goal 2 then would be repeated to determine if the resulting equilibrium point, (P_e, Q_e), lay above or below point f; the appropriate t would be selected depending on this result, again as in Goal 2.

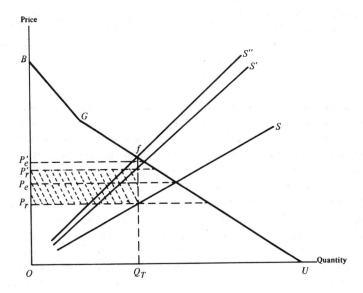

FIGURE 8

Following these steps first requires differentiating equation (4.21), which gives a necessary condition for the maximum T.

$$\frac{dT}{dt} = TR + t\,\frac{dTR}{dt} = 0,$$

which, upon substitution of $P_e Q_e$ for TR, becomes

$$\frac{dT}{dt} = P_e Q_e + t\,\frac{dTR}{dt} = 0. \tag{4.22}$$

Substituting (4.20) into (4.22) results in

$$\frac{dT}{dt} = P_e Q_e + t\,\frac{P_e Q_e g}{(1-t)}(\eta + 1) = 0;$$

$$= \left[1 + g\left(\frac{t}{1-t}\right)(\eta + 1)\right] P_e Q_e = 0;$$

which divided by $P_e Q_e$ yields

$$-1 = g\left(\frac{t}{1-t}\right)(\eta + 1); \qquad g = \frac{\epsilon}{\epsilon - \eta} > 0;\; 0 \leqslant t < 1. \tag{4.23}$$

Compared with the necessary condition for maximum total revenue (Goal 2), this condition is more complicated, particularly since the term denoted by g includes both the supply and demand elasticities. However, since g and $t/(1-$

t) are both strictly positive for any t between zero and one, dividing by $gt/(1-t)$ yields

$$(\eta + 1) = - \frac{(1-t)}{gt} . \tag{4.24}$$

The right-hand side of (4.24), therefore, always is strictly negative, which requires that η be strictly less than minus one. Compared with the condition for optimal t under the previous goal of maximizing total revenue, this indicates that the unconstrained maximization of tax revenue requires that the supply function intersect the combined demand function somewhere *above* the point of unitary elasticity.

If the point of unitary elasticity lay at point f or above, then the optimal t would be that which satisfied equation (4.23). If the point of unitary elasticity were below point f, then certainly the optimal tax would be at least high enough to shift the supply function to S'' in Figure 8. If the point of unitary elasticity were below but quite near point f, then it is possible that the optimal t still would be such that the supply function would be shifted above S'' somewhat, since (4.23) is satisfied only if the elasticity of demand is greater (in absolute terms) than one. In all cases, however, Goal 3 will call for a tax at least as high as would Goal 2. Further, whenever Goal 2 would require that the supply function be shifted above S'', that is, whenever the point of unitary elasticity of the combined demand function is above point f, then Goal 3 would require a higher t than would Goal 2.

In actual practice, of course, there are insufficient data to optimize in the fashion being suggested here. Even if all the necessary data were available to identify exactly the functions involved, it probably would be politically naive to attempt to optimize tax revenue expressly in this fashion. Moreover, as will be suggested below by some examples, the tax rates indicated by such goal optimizing behavior might be very high, higher than would be politically acceptable, even if they were economically justifiable. Nevertheless, this analysis allows us to make a judgment as to the direction of change of tax rates with a change between Goals 2 and 3: switching from Goal 2 to Goal 3 would, at a minimum, leave tax rates unchanged and probably would call for higher tax rates.

**Goal 4: Maximization
of Interstate Tax Revenue**

The possibility of seeking the goal of maximum tax revenue from without the state is perhaps the most interesting of the four goals being considered. Although it is not possible constitutionally to charge different tax rates for gas sold interstate, it still is possible to maximize the tax revenue from the "foreigner" by choosing the correct level for t. This goal obviously raises important questions regarding intergovernmental relations and interstate redistribution of income, questions which will be considered further in chapter 7.

As when pursuing Goals 2 and 3, pursuit of Goal 4 also will call for a tax which shifts the supply function upward until any excess demand that existed initially is eliminated entirely. With a shift of the supply function of this magnitude, the regulated price and the equilibrium price in the absence of regulation are equal. The intersection point of the demand and the shifted supply functions which meets this condition is again indicated by f in Figure 9. The upward shift in the supply function which maximizes interstate tax revenue necessarily would be at least to the indicated level for the supply function because, until this level is reached, P_r, Q_2, and t all are increasing, where Q_2 refers to the amount of gas sold in the interstate market. The increase in Q_2 with the rise in $P_r' = P_e'$ was demonstrated above and also can be observed by reference to Figure 9. With the gross value of interstate sales denoted by TR_2 and interstate tax revenue from those sales by T_2, when the supply function is shifted above S' in Figure 9 we have

$$TR_2 = P_e \times Q_2 \qquad\qquad (4.25)$$

and

$$T_2 = t \times TR_2 = t \times P_e \times Q_2. \qquad\qquad (4.26)$$

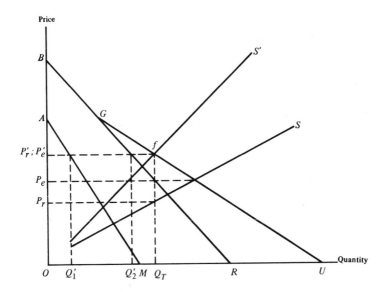

FIGURE 9

The same procedure followed under Goals 2 and 3 will be employed again to determine if the optimal tax is that which results in a shift of the supply function to point f, or if the tax should be even higher. Letting the interstate demand equation be expressed by

$$P = a_2 + b_2 Q_2 \tag{4.27}$$

then

$$Q_2 = \frac{P_e - a_2}{b_2} . \tag{4.28}$$

Substituting (4.28) into (4.26), the revenue from interstate sales is given by

$$T_2 = t \times P_e(P_e - a_2) / b_2 . \tag{4.29}$$

This gives rise to the following first order condition for the optimum t:

$$\frac{dT_2}{dt} = \frac{P_e(P_e - a_2)}{b_2} + t\left[\frac{dP_e}{dt}\left(\frac{P_e - a_2}{b_2}\right) + \frac{P_e}{b_2}\frac{dP_e}{dt}\right] = 0;$$

$$\frac{dT_2}{dt} = P_e(P_e - a_2) + t\,\frac{dP_e}{dt}\,(2P_e - a_2) = 0. \tag{4.30}$$

Substituting from (4.19) and (4.28), where $g = \epsilon/(\epsilon - \eta)$,

$$\frac{dT_2}{dt} = P_e(b_2 Q_2) + \frac{tP_e g}{(1-t)}\,[P_e + P_e - a_2] = 0;$$

$$\frac{dT_2}{dt} = \left[b_2 Q_2 + g\left(\frac{t}{1-t}\right)(P_e + b_2 Q_2)\right] P_e = 0. \tag{4.31}$$

As in (4.17), one may write

$$b_2 = \frac{1}{\eta_2}\frac{P_e}{Q_2} . \tag{4.32}$$

Substituting this into (4.31),

$$\frac{dT_2}{dt} = \left[\frac{1}{\eta_2}\frac{P_e}{Q_2} Q_2 + g\left(\frac{t}{1-t}\right)\left(P_e + \frac{1}{\eta_2}\frac{P_e}{Q_2} Q_2\right)\right] P_e = 0$$

$$= \left[1 + g\left(\frac{t}{1-t}\right)(\eta_2 + 1)\right]\frac{P_e^2}{\eta_2} = 0.$$

Dividing by $P_e{}^2/\eta_2$ gives the necessary condition for optimal t under Goal 4:

$$-1 = g \left(\frac{t}{1-t}\right)(\eta_2 + 1), \tag{4.33}$$

where η_2 is the elasticity of demand in the interstate market.

Using the same reasoning as under Goal 3, following (4.23), this result implies that $\eta_2 < -1$. In the usual terminology, this would call for the state to establish a production tax such that the industry would be operating somewhere in the elastic portion of the interstate demand function if tax revenue from out of state were to be maximized.

This result, that the optimal tax under Goal 4 requires that the price line intersect the interstate demand function above the point of unitary elasticity, parallels that obtained under Goal 3 for the *total* demand function. Since under Goal 4 attention is focused on the interstate demand function, while under Goal 3 it is the elasticity of the combined demand function which is critical, the two results, although analogous, are not directly comparable in terms of the absolute level of tax required in order to maximize the respective goal functions.

One way to make such a comparison is the following: assume that initially Goal 3 is in effect. That is, the tax already has been adjusted so that the tax revenue from *both* markets combined is being maximized. To avoid the trivial case, assume that maximization of Goal 3 involved shifting the supply function above S' in Figure 9 so that under this optimal tax the point on the demand function where the supply function intersects it is above point f. Denote this point by $(P_e{}^*, Q_e{}^*)$. The expression for the necessary condition to be fulfilled when it is desired to maximize interstate tax revenue, namely (4.33), then will be compared with the one obtained under Goal 3 (4.23); the implication for the level of the production tax of changing from Goal 3 to Goal 4 then will evolve. Some additional operations are necessary before the comparison can be made, however, since (4.33), unlike (4.23), contains η_2 explicitly.

If α_1 and α_2 represent the proportion of sales in the intrastate and interstate markets respectively, then

$$\alpha_2 = 1-\alpha_1. \tag{4.34}$$

In addition, it is necessary to have a relationship between the elasticity of demand of each of the two separate demand functions and the elasticity of demand of the combined demand function, all at the same price, with no excess demand. This relationship is

$$\eta = \alpha_1 \eta_1 + \alpha_2 \eta_2.{}^2 \tag{4.35}$$

---

[2] A proof of this relationship is given in Appendix 1.

Substituting (4.34) into (4.35),

$$\eta = \eta_2 + \alpha_1 (\eta_1 - \eta_2).\tag{4.36}$$

Let t^* be the optimal level of the production tax when total tax revenue is being maximized (Goal 3). That is, t^* satisfies the necessary condition as expressed in (4.23). Substituting (4.36) into (4.23) gives

$$-1 = g \left(\frac{t^*}{1-t^*} \right) [(\eta_2 + 1) + \alpha_1 (\eta_1 - \eta_2)],\tag{4.37}$$

or, equivalently,

$$-1 = g \left(\frac{t^*}{1-t^*} \right) (\eta_2 + 1) + \alpha_1 g \left(\frac{t^*}{1-t^*} \right) (\eta_1 - \eta_2).\tag{4.38}$$

Equation (4.38) is merely a transformed version of the necessary condition for an optimal tax under Goal 3, being derived by substitution of (4.36) into (4.23), as indicated. If η_1 and η_2 are equal, (4.38) reduces to (4.33), hence Goals 3 and 4 would call for the same optimum t.

Consider the case where η_2 is greater in absolute value than η_1, that is, where interstate demand is the more elastic of the two. With Goal 3 already in effect, the tax would be at the value represented by t^*, satisfying (4.38). A switch to Goal 4 would necessitate selecting a new value of t which would satisfy (4.33). The difference between (4.38) and (4.33) is that (4.38) contains an extra term on the right-hand side, namely $\alpha_1 g (1-t^*)(\eta_1 - \eta_2)$. Switching from Goal 3 to 4, in terms of the necessary condition for the optimal tax, thus involves eliminating the last term on the right from (4.38). But observe that this term, $\alpha_1 g t^*(\eta_1 - \eta_2)/(1-t^*)$, is positive, given that $(\eta_1 - \eta_2)$, α_1, and t^* all are strictly positive, since g is also positive. Subtracting this term from the right-hand side of (4.38) gives rise to

$$-1 > g \left(\frac{t^*}{1-t^*} \right) (\eta_2 + 1),\tag{4.39}$$

an inequality, due to the fact that the tax is still at the level which satisfies (4.38), namely t^*. Since adoption of Goal 4 would require satisfying equation (4.33), it would be necessary to make the right-hand side of (4.39) less negative. To determine in which direction t should be moved, the sign of the derivative with respect to t of

$$F = g \left(\frac{t}{1-t} \right) (\eta_2 + 1)\tag{4.40}$$

will be found. Replacing g by $\epsilon/(\epsilon - \eta)$ and using equations (4.15) and (4.17), F can be reduced to

$$F = \frac{bt}{b(1-t)-B}\ (\eta_2 + 1),\tag{4.41}$$

from which is obtained

$$\frac{dF}{dt} = (\eta_2 + 1)\ \frac{d}{dt}\left[\frac{bt}{b(1-t)-B}\right] + \left[\frac{bt}{b(1-t)-B}\right]\frac{d(\eta_2+1)}{dt},$$

$$\overset{(-)}{= (\eta_2 + 1)}\ \overset{(+)}{\left[\frac{b[b(1-t)-B]+b^2t}{[b(1-t)-B]^2}\right]} + \overset{(+)}{\left[\frac{bt}{b(1-t)-B}\right]}\overset{(-)}{\frac{d(\eta_2+1)}{dt}}.$$

It then can be seen that dF/dt is negative, given the signs of the individual parts of the expression which follow from previous assumptions on the parameters. This result requires that if t is *reduced* slightly from t^*, the value of F would *increase*, which is to say that F would become less negative. In other words, since at t^* F was less than minus one, *decreasing* t would tend towards satisfying (4.33), the desired condition under Goal 4. This means moving to a less elastic point on the interstate demand curve.

The magnitude of the required adjustment of t depends on the magnitude of the term that was eliminated from (4.38) when switching from the necessary condition under Goal 3 to that for Goal 4. An idea of the relative size of the change in t therefore can be obtained by looking at this term $-\alpha_1 g\left(\frac{t^*}{1-t^*}\right)(\eta_2-\eta_2)$. Replacing g by $\epsilon/(\epsilon-\eta)$, and substituting equation (4.35) for η, the following identity holds:

$$\alpha_1 g\left(\frac{t^*}{1-t^*}\right)(\eta_1-\eta_2) \equiv \alpha_1\left(\frac{\epsilon}{\epsilon-\eta_2-\alpha_1(\eta_1-\eta_2)}\right)\left(\frac{t^*}{1-t^*}\right)(\eta_1-\eta_2)$$

$$\equiv \alpha_1\left(\frac{\epsilon t^*}{1-t^*}\right)\frac{1}{\frac{\epsilon-\eta_2}{(\eta_1-\eta_2)}-\alpha_1}.\tag{4.42}$$

From (4.42) it can be seen that this term is larger for large values of α_1 and for large differences between the intrastate and interstate elasticities of demand, $(\eta_1-\eta_2)$. In general, the larger are α_1 and $(\eta_1-\eta_2)$, the greater is the required change in t in going from Goal 3 to Goal 4.

If $(\eta_1-\eta_2)$ were negative, that is, if at the equilibrium position resulting from maximizing Goal 3 the intrastate demand was *more* elastic than the interstate demand, switching from Goal 3 to Goal 4 would require an *increase* in t to some level above t^*.

In sum, the magnitude of the production tax which maximizes interstate tax revenue could be either higher or lower than that tax which maximizes tax revenue from both interstate and intrastate sales, depending on the relative elasticity of the separate demand functions. The optimal tax for Goal 4 could sometimes be less than that for Goal 2, but only under the rather perverse situation that most of the gas flowed into an extremely inelastic intrastate market rather than into a very elastic interstate market. Optimal taxes under Goals 3 and 4 generally will be considerably higher than under Goal 2, as will be shown below when some specific examples are presented.

Producing State Goals
and Optimal Severance Taxes

Comparisons now might profitably be drawn among the various producing state goals considered and the optimal tax which results from pursuit of those goals.

One factor is clear from the model: with an effective price ceiling the intrastate demand is satisfied at approximately the regulated price at the expense of gas supplies which otherwise would flow into interstate commerce. A tax policy resulting in a lower observed regulated price thus favors intrastate consumption while one leading to higher regulated prices (whether or not the return flows to productive factors) results in a higher proportion of gas going to interstate consumers. Similarly, higher state severance taxes lead not only to higher revenues to the state but also to a higher proportion of those revenues being derived from interstate customers, as long as the quantity of gas supplied is not affected by the change in tax rate. When the level of tax does affect the quantity supplied, the proportion of tax revenue from the interstate market increases or decreases depending upon whether or not the elasticity of interstate demand is less than or greater than the elasticity of the intrastate demand. The optimal tax policy for a state following Goal 1 thus is exactly opposite that of the same state choosing Goal 4.

A further general conclusion arising from the model is that the state *at least* would increase tax to what we have termed point f if it followed Goals 2, 3, or 4. Until non-market allocation is eliminated, an increase in the tax rate leaves the level of output unchanged; leaves the return to gas suppliers—including both factor owners and rental income recipients— unchanged; increases tax revenue to the state; and increases both absolutely and relatively the tax receipts paid by non-state citizens.

Beyond point f the picture becomes more mixed because higher tax rates then bring restrictions on quantity supplied (declines in levels of output) and hence declines in employment and in return to rental elements. Declines in levels of output, however, do lower levels of costs, which is another way of saying that resources are freed to perform other tasks with higher private and social utility. Rational policy making would consider the alternative uses of resources consumed to obtain gas tax revenue, and this consideration would increase the motive for sometimes raising taxes beyond point f, with the actual level selected dependent upon the particular functions and the choice of goal or goals.

In summary, it is clear that cost-based regulation of the form chosen by the FPC opens an opportunity for producing states to achieve a number of goals, the range and complexity of which only have been suggested here. The producing state's opportunity to benefit from effecting Goals 2, 3, and 4 is directly related to the magnitude of the gap existing between the regulated price and the price at which excess demand is eliminated. The following chapter examines in absolute terms the potential results of adoption of Goals 2, 3, and 4, given various, somewhat reasonable assumptions regarding the variables.

5

Optimal Tax Determination: Texas and Louisiana

Some of the implications of the preceding portions of this book now will be made less abstract through an illustrative application of the field market model to data describing the situation in Texas and Louisiana in 1967. Some actual data—prices, quantities, and production taxes—are used, together with alternative estimates of the difference between the regulated and the equilibrium prices and postulated elasticities of the various functions. Average value at the wellhead was used as the price variable. Given this information, optimal taxes can be calculated in the manner already discussed. Imprecise data, difficulties of definition, and the use of a comparative static model all combine to render these quantitative results only suggestive. Should there be disagreement as to the values chosen for the parameters, or should updated results be desired, other estimates can be made by the reader using the procedures outlined.

A caution might be suggested to the reader interpreting the results of applying this model: the model deals with the long run, which means that effectively it deals with new gas supplies and with demand not satisfied by already committed reserves. Hence, the immediate effect of an increase in the tax rate would not be the same as it would be after adjustments had taken place. The answers given here reflect the post-adjustment results. The significance of this difference is apparent when one realizes that for the individual producer without a severance tax clause in his gas sales contract the immediate effect of a tax increase on flowing gas is a reduction in the producer's income, no matter what happens to ceiling price. Despite its long-run nature, at least the *direction* of industry change associated with moving to a different policy is predicted by this model even in the short run.

It has been assumed that prior to any policy action excess demand existed in the interstate markets. Since this assumption implies that the observed price in a given state then would be approximately equal to the weighted interstate ceiling price, the initial regulated price, P_r, was assumed to be equal to the average price at the wellhead. This assumption is realistic over the long run, but is subject to the short-run uncertainties alluded to above. The remainder of the variables are rather straightforward and require no elaboration.

Calculation of the Estimates

The actual calculations, the results of which are found in Tables IA, IB, IIA, and IIB, were accomplished with the aid of a computer, but for clarity and simplicity the discussion here is in terms of Figure 10. Precise algebraic manipulations and arithmetic calculations are unnecessary for understanding.[1] From information in the *Minerals Yearbook,* point q was plotted.[2] This represents the average wellhead price, P_r, and total sales, Q_T. Point w gives the price-quantity point for intrastate sales, ignoring any differences between intrastate and interstate prices as merely adjusting for specific regulatory and other conditions associated with the fact of "intrastatedness." Under the assumption of excess demand, q lies on the supply function. Assuming, for simplicity, that the long-run elasticity of supply is unity, the result is the straight-line approximation to the supply function, line S, passing through the origin. An assumption on the elasticity of intrastate demand at point w allows the drawing of a linear approximation to this demand function, represented in Figure 10 by line D_1.

The next step, following the procedure used in calculating the sample results given below, was to judge how much the average price would rise if the ceiling price were removed and long-run adjustments were made. That is, a hypothetical difference between P_e and P_r was selected. Arriving at a value for this discrepancy allows plotting the equilibrium price-quantity point on the supply function, since such an equilibrium point would be found at the intersection of the supply and combined intrastate and interstate demand curves. This point is denoted by e. Finally, making an assumption regarding the value of the elasticity of the aggregate demand function at point e permits drawing in the straight-line approximation to this function, D_T. From the equations for D_1 and D_T it then is possible to derive and plot D_2, the interstate demand function.

---

[1] Development of the equations used in working out the examples and the computer program (in FOCAL) used in estimating the optimal tax rates will be supplied upon request.

[2] Data for the 1967 year were chosen for these sample calculations because there was a change in definition in 1968 which would create difficulty in the interstate-intrastate breakdown. *Minerals Yearbook,* 1967, vol. I-II, Table 2, p. 759.

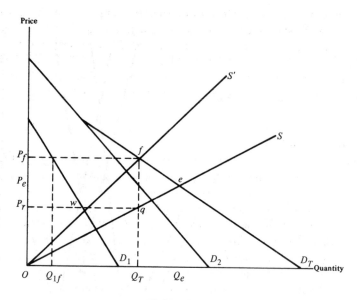

FIGURE 10

Performing the above for particular values of P_r, Q_T, and so forth, permits calculating the required levels of the production tax necessary to attain any one of the goals discussed in chapter 4. It also is possible to calculate the level of tax required to shift S so that it passes through point f, the maximum value the tax could take without reducing total sales. The price at this point is denoted by P_f, with Q_{1f} sold intrastate, and Q_T minus Q_{1f} sold interstate.

Results of the Calculations

The procedure outlined above was carried out for Texas and Louisiana, using information taken from *Minerals Yearbook* for 1967 together with a range of values for the assumed data. The results are presented in Tables IA and IB, with some of the results also shown in Figures 11 and 12. Consider these two figures. The lines designated by S are the original supply functions (assuming unitary elasticity) incorporating an initial production tax of 12.43 percent for Louisiana and 6.82 percent for Texas. The lines designated by $S(G2)$ represent the supply function shifted upward until it intersects the demand function at point f. Under the set of assumptions for the case illustrated, this coincides with the supply function shifted optimally under Goal 2, since under the elasticity assumption chosen the point of unitary elasticity lies to the right of point f. The line designated by $S(G3)$ represents the supply function which has been shifted by increasing t to the optimal value when pursuing Goal 3. The same is true for the line $S(G4)$ with reference

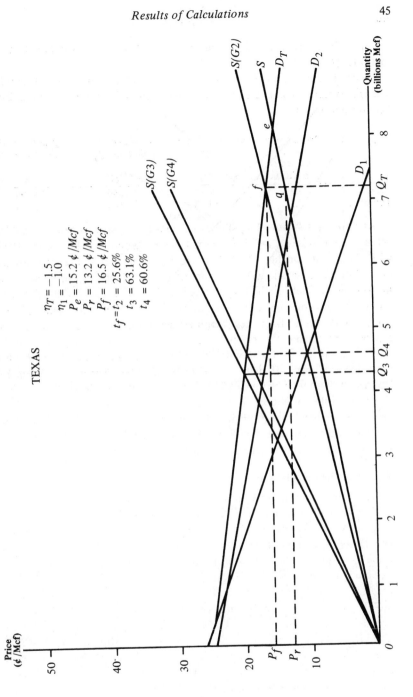

FIGURE 11

to Goal 4. The case depicted in Figures 11 and 12 corresponds to line thirteen of Tables IA and IB.

Figure 11 and Tables IA and IIA pertain to Texas; Figure 12 and Tables IB and IIB to Louisiana. The observed, or initial, data for 1967 are summarized here for convenience.

	Average value at the wellhead (P_r)	*Initial production tax*	*Total quantity produced (Q_T)*	*Quantity sold interstate (Q_2)*
	(¢/Mcf)	*(%)*	*(M^3Mcf)*	*(M^3Mcf)*
Texas	13.2	6.82	7.1889	3.4794
Louisiana	18.5	12.43	5.7169	4.5734

As noted in footnote b of Tables IIA and IIB, approximately $66 million actually were received by Texas in natural gas production tax during 1967, with about half, roughly $32 million, coming from gas sold interstate. Similar quantities for Louisiana were $113 million and $90 million, the higher totals in Louisiana reflecting a higher tax rate and the greater proportion of gas sold interstate. All of the estimates appearing in Tables IIA and IIB are considerably greater than these amounts, so regardless of the goal chosen the estimated attainable tax revenue was always higher than the observed tax revenue. Even those amounts of production tax revenues obtainable through a tax increase just sufficient to eliminate the excess demand, t_f, are higher than those revenues existing in 1967, as can be seen from the tables.

These results, of course, are not surprising given the existence of positive excess demand, but what might be surprising is the rate of increase in tax revenue with an increase in t. The selling price equals the regulated price, P_r, and, since the total quantity sold is constant, the tax revenue is

$$T = t \times P_r \times Q_T \ .$$

Recalling that $P_r = C/(1-t)$, where C reflects all factors entering into the price other than the production tax, we have

$$P = CQ_T \left(\frac{t}{1-t} \right).$$

From this equation we see that, given excess demand, the numerator of the expression increases while the denominator decreases, both effects working to increase tax revenue. Even beyond the point where the equilibrium quantity sold decreases (that is, above point f in the previous diagrams) tax revenue may continue to increase. Thus, t_f in Tables IA and IB (column 5) takes on values ranging from 25 to 60 percent, while t_3 and t_4, the tax rates for Goals 3 and 4, exceed 75 percent in several cases for the selected data.

It is interesting to compare the size of the potential production tax revenues, as calculated, with the observed actual state total tax revenue, including all taxes. Tax revenue for Louisiana, again for the year 1967, was

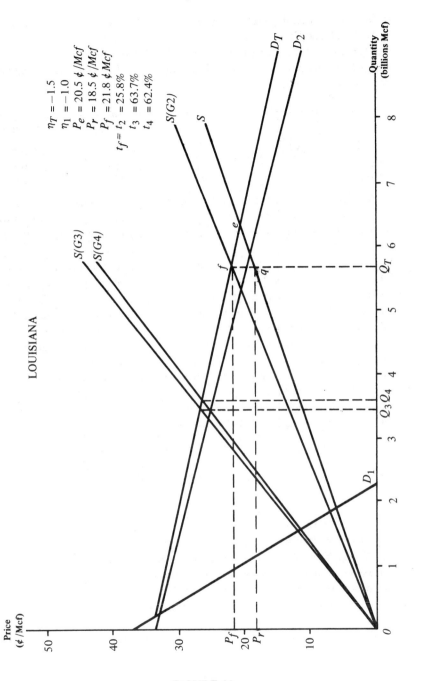

FIGURE 12

Table IA

**Optimal Severance Tax Rate and Its Effects, Selected Goals,
Various Assumptions: Texas**

	Assumed values			*Maximum tax, zero quantity change[f]*				*Results for optimal tax under Goal 2*			
Elasticity, inter-state demand[c]	*Elasticity, com-bined demand[d]*	*Equilibrium price[e]*	*Tax rate*	*Price with tax t_f*	*Observed quan-tity produced[g]*	*Percentage sold interstate*		*Tax rate, Goal 2*	*Price with tax t_2*	*Quantity pro-duced*	*Percentage sold interstate*
$-\eta_1$	$-\eta_T$	P_e	t_f	P_f	Q_T			t_2	P_2	Q_{2T}	
		¢/Mcf	%	¢/Mcf	M^3Mcf			%	¢/Mcf	M^3Mcf	
(1)	*(2)*	*(3)*	*(4)*	*(5)*	*(6)*	*(7)*	*(8)*	*(9)*	*(10)*	*(11)*	*(12)*
1	0.5	0.5	15.2	35.9	19.2	7.1889	60.1	53.4	22.8	6.2093	62.0
2	0.5	0.5	17.2	51.2	25.2	7.1889	71.9	53.4	25.8	7.0263	72.4
3	0.5	0.5	19.2	60.6	31.2	7.1889	83.6	60.6[b]	31.2[b]	7.1889[b]	83.6[b]
4	0.5	1.0	15.2	28.5	17.2	7.1889	56.2	28.5[b]	17.2[b]	7.1889[b]	56.2[b]
5	0.5	1.0	17.2	42.0	21.2	7.1889	64.1	42.0[b]	21.2[b]	7.1889[b]	64.1[b]
6	0.5	1.0	19.2	51.2	25.2	7.1889	71.9	51.2[b]	25.2[b]	7.1889[b]	71.9[b]
7	0.5	1.5	15.2	25.6	16.5	7.1889	54.9	25.6[b]	16.5[b]	7.1889[b]	54.9[b]
8	0.5	1.5	17.2	38.1	19.9	7.1889	61.5	38.1[b]	19.9[b]	7.1889[b]	61.5[b]
9	0.5	1.5	19.2	47.0	23.2	7.1889	68.0	47.0[b]	23.2[b]	7.1889[b]	68.0[b]
10	1.0	1.0	15.2	28.5	17.2	7.1889	64.1	28.5[b]	17.2[b]	7.1889[b]	64.1[b]
11	1.0	1.0	17.2	42.0	21.2	7.1889	79.7	42.0[b]	21.2[b]	7.1889[b]	79.7[b]
12	1.0	1.0	19.2	51.2	25.2	7.1889	95.3	51.2[b]	25.2[b]	7.1889[b]	95.3[b]
13	1.0	1.5	15.2	25.6	16.5	7.1889	61.3	25.6[b]	16.5[b]	7.1889[b]	61.3[b]
14	1.0	1.5	17.2	38.1	19.9	7.1889	74.6	38.1[b]	19.9[b]	7.1889[b]	74.6[b]
15	1.0	1.5	19.2	47.0	23.2	7.1889	87.5	47.0[b]	23.2[b]	7.1889[b]	87.5[b]
16	1.5	1.5	15.2	25.6	16.5	7.1889	67.7	25.6[b]	16.5[b]	7.1889[b]	67.7[b]
17	1.5	1.5	17.2	38.1	19.9	7.1889	87.7	38.1[b]	19.9[b]	7.1889[b]	87.7[b]
18	1.5	1.5	19.2	47.0	23.2	7.1889	100.0	47.0[b]	23.2[b]	7.1889[b]	100.0[b]

[a]Optimal tax would eliminate all sales in intrastate market.

[b]Optimal tax same as t_f (the point of unitary elasticity of the combined demand function is below point f—see discussion, pp. 27-28).

[c]Values assumed for η_1 evaluated at the observed price under regulation (P_f) and the observed intrastate sales (Q_1). (See tables in Appendix 2 for the observed data used in the examples and sources. These data include values for intrastate sales, total sales, average value at the wellhead, and initial production tax.)

Table IA (cont.)

	Results for optimal tax under Goal 3				Results for optimal tax under Goal 4			
	Tax rate, Goal 3	Price with tax t_3	Quantity produced	Percentage sold interstate	Tax rate, Goal 4	Price with tax t_4	Quantity produced	Percentage sold interstate
	t_3 %	P_3 ¢/Mcf	Q_{3T} M^3Mcf		t_4 %	P_4 ¢/Mcf	Q_{4T} M^3Mcf	
	(13)	(14)	(15)	(16)	(17)	(18)	(19)	(20)
1	75.8	30.0	4.2449	68.3	82.6	33.2	3.3765	73.4
2	75.8	34.0	4.8035	83.5	_a	_a	_a	_a
3	75.8	37.9	5.3620	95.6	_a	_a	_a	_a
4	67.4	22.5	4.2911	44.1	57.8	20.9	5.1609	49.2
5	67.4	25.5	4.8557	59.2	62.8	24.6	5.3454	60.6
6	67.4	28.5	5.4203	71.1	66.5	28.3	5.5304	71.2
7	63.1	20.0	4.3225	36.4	49.0	18.6	5.5326	46.6
8	63.1	22.7	4.8913	51.4	53.8	21.6	5.8178	56.4
9	63.1	25.3	5.4600	63.3	57.4	24.5	6.1064	65.3
10	67.4	22.5	4.2911	74.6	78.3	24.7	3.1274	84.4
11	67.4	25.5	4.8557	94.7	_a	_a	_a	_a
12	_a	_a	_a	_a	_a	_a	_a	_a
13	63.1	20.0	4.3225	58.7	60.6	19.8	4.5510	59.0
14	63.1	22.7	4.8913	78.6	67.6	23.3	4.4070	80.0
15	63.1	25.3	5.4600	94.4	_a	_a	_a	_a
16	63.1	20.0	4.3225	80.9	77.5	21.8	2.8696	97.4
17	_a	_a	_a	_a	_a	_a	_a	_a
18	_a	_a	_a	_a	_a	_a	_a	_a

dValues assumed for η_T at the point defined by P_e (column 4) and the quantity Q_e; Q_e is determined from the supply function through the observed point (P_r, Q_T), derived as explained in the text, applying P_e.

eThree different values, two, four, and six cents respectively, above the observed average price at the wellhead (P_r). P_r obtained from *Minerals Yearbook*, 1967, vol. I-II, Table 2, p.759.

fTax required to shift the supply function sufficiently to eliminate the excess demand.

gFrom *Minerals Yearbook*, 1967, vol. I-II, Table 2, p. 759.

Table IB

**Optimal Severance Tax Rate and Its Effects, Selected Goals,
Various Assumptions: Louisiana[h]**

	Assumed values			Maximum tax, zero quantity change[f]				Results for optimal tax under Goal 2			
Elasticity, interstate demand[c]	*Elasticity, combined demand[d]*	*Equilibrium price[e]*	*Tax rate*	*Price with tax t_f*	*Observed quantity produced[g]*	*Percentage sold interstate*	*Tax rate, Goal 2*	*Price with tax t_2*	*Quantity produced*	*Percentage sold interstate*
$-\eta_1$	$-\eta_T$	P_e ¢/Mcf	t_f %	P_f ¢/Mcf	Q_T M^3Mcf		t_2 %	P_2 ¢/Mcf	Q_{2T} M^3Mcf	
(1)	*(2)*	*(3)*	*(4)*	*(5)*	*(6)*	*(7)*	*(8)*	*(9)*	*(10)*	*(11)*	*(12)*
1	0.5	0.5	20.5	33.9	24.5	5.7169	83.2	56.2	30.8	4.7520	83.9
2	0.5	0.5	22.5	46.9	30.5	5.7169	86.5	56.2	33.8	5.2156	87.1
3	0.5	0.5	24.5	55.6	36.5	5.7169	89.7	56.2	36.7	5.6792	89.8
4	0.5	1.0	20.5	28.0	22.5	5.7169	82.2	28.9[b]	22.5[b]	5.7169[b]	82.2[b]
5	0.5	1.0	22.5	38.9	26.5	5.7169	84.3	38.9[b]	26.5[b]	5.7169[b]	84.3[b]
6	0.5	1.0	24.5	46.9	30.5	5.7169	86.5	46.9[b]	30.5[b]	5.7169[b]	86.5[b]
7	0.5	1.5	20.5	25.8	21.8	5.7169	81.8	25.8[b]	21.8[b]	5.7169[b]	81.8[b]
8	0.5	1.5	22.5	35.6	25.2	5.7169	83.6	35.6[b]	25.2[b]	5.7169[b]	83.6[b]
9	0.5	1.5	24.5	43.2	28.5	5.7169	85.4	43.2[b]	28.5[b]	5.7169[b]	85.4[b]
10	1.0	1.0	20.5	28.0	22.5	5.7169	84.3	28.0[b]	22.5[b]	5.7169[b]	84.3[b]
11	1.0	1.0	22.5	38.9	26.5	5.7169	88.6	38.9[b]	26.5[b]	5.7169[b]	88.6[b]
12	1.0	1.0	24.5	46.9	30.5	5.7169	93.0	46.9[b]	30.5[b]	5.7169[b]	93.0[b]
13	1.0	1.5	20.5	25.8	21.8	5.7169	83.6	25.8[b]	21.8[b]	5.7169[b]	83.6[b]
14	1.0	1.5	22.5	35.6	25.2	5.7169	87.2	35.6[b]	25.2[b]	5.7169[b]	87.2[b]
15	1.0	1.5	24.5	43.2	28.5	5.7169	90.8	43.2[b]	28.5[b]	5.7169[b]	90.8[b]
16	1.5	1.5	20.5	25.8	21.8	5.7169	85.4	25.8[b]	21.8[b]	5.7169[b]	85.4[b]
17	1.5	1.5	22.5	35.6	25.2	5.7169	90.9	35.6[b]	25.2[b]	5.7169[b]	90.9[b]
18	1.5	1.5	24.5	43.2	28.5	5.7169	96.2	43.2[b]	28.5[b]	5.7169[b]	96.2[b]

[a]Optimal tax would eliminate all sales in intrastate market.

[b]Optimal tax same as t_f (the point of unitary elasticity of the combined demand function is below point f–see discussion, pp. 27-28).

[c]Values assumed for η_1 evaluated at the observed price under regulation (P_f) and the observed intrastate sales (Q_1). (See tables in Appendix 2 for the observed data used in the examples and sources. These data include values for intrastate sales, total sales, average value at the wellhead, and initial production tax.)

[d]Values assumed for η_T at the point defined by P_e (column 4) and the quantity Q_e; Q_e is determined from the supply function through the observed point (P_r, Q_T), derived as explained in the text, applying P_e.

Table IB (cont.)

	Results for optimal tax under Goal 3				Results for optimal tax under Goal 4			
	Tax rate, Goal 3 t_3 %	Price with tax t_3 P_3 ¢/Mcf	Quantity produced Q_{3T} M^3Mcf	Percentage sold interstate	Tax rate, Goal 4 t_4 %	Price with tax t_4 P_4 ¢/Mcf	Quantity produced Q_{4T} M^3Mcf	Percentage sold interstate
	(13)	(14)	(15)	(16)	(17)	(18)	(19)	(20)
1	76.6	40.1	3.3096	85.6	77.8	40.8	3.1970	85.8
2	76.6	44.0	3.6325	90.2	78.0	45.5	3.4024	90.9
3	76.6	47.9	3.9554	94.1	79.6	50.1	3.6095	95.4
4	68.1	30.1	3.3830	76.8	64.8	29.3	3.6326	77.7
5	68.1	33.0	3.7131	81.3	66.0	32.4	3.8891	81.7
6	68.1	35.9	4.0431	85.0	66.9	35.6	4.1535	85.2
7	63.7	26.8	3.4290	74.1	58.8	26.0	3.7814	75.9
8	63.7	29.4	3.7636	78.6	60.0	28.8	4.0576	79.6
9	63.7	32.0	4.0981	82.3	60.9	31.5	4.3417	82.9
10	68.1	30.1	3.3830	87.3	70.1	30.6	3.2249	87.7
11	68.1	33.0	3.7131	93.3	71.6	34.0	3.4054	94.5
12	68.1	35.9	4.0431	98.3	_a	_a	_a	_a
13	63.7	26.8	3.4290	81.6	62.4	26.6	3.5245	81.7
14	63.7	29.4	3.7636	87.5	64.0	29.4	3.7392	87.5
15	63.7	32.0	4.0981	92.4	65.3	32.3	3.9552	92.7
16	63.7	26.8	3.4290	89.0	66.3	27.2	3.2336	89.6
17	63.7	29.4	3.7636	96.4	68.4	30.2	3.3708	98.4
18	_a	_a	_a	_a	_a	_a	_a	_a

eThree different values, two, four, and six cents respectively, above the observed average price at the wellhead (P_r). P_r obtained from *Minerals Yearbook,* 1967, vol. I-II, Table 2, p. 759.

fTax required to shift the supply function sufficiently to eliminate the excess demand.

gFrom *Minerals Yearbook,* 1967, vol. I-II, Table 2, p. 759.

hEstimates were made for Louisiana on the basis that all Louisiana production was subject to state severance taxation, including that from the federal domain. This simplifying convention in part reflects reality because of the practice of granting a somewhat higher price for gas in the federal domain off-shore to compensate for the costlier operations there. For the period in question approximately 14 percent of the gas was non-taxable. See footnote *c,* Table 4, Appendix 2.

Table IIA

Calculated Tax Revenue from Selected Policies: Texas[b]
(millions of dollars)

	Maximum tax, zero quantity change		Goal 2 (maximum total revenue)		Goal 3 (maximum tax revenue)		Goal 4 (maximum interstate tax revenue)	
	$Total^c$	$Inter\text{-}state^d$	$Total^c$	$Inter\text{-}state^d$	$Total^c$	$Inter\text{-}state^d$	$Total^c$	$Inter\text{-}state^d$
1	496	298	593	367	965	659	966	680
2	928	667	968	701	1238	1034	—a	—a
3	1359	1136	1359	1136	1540	1473	—a	—a
4	352	198	352	198	651	287	623	307
5	640	410	640	410	835	494	826	500
6	928	667	928	667	1041	740	1041	741
7	304	167	304	167	545	199	504	235
8	545	335	545	335	701	360	676	381
9	784	533	784	533	872	552	859	561
10	352	226	352	226	651	485	605	510
11	640	510	640	510	835	790	—a	—a
12	928	884	928	884	—a	—a	—a	—a
13	304	186	304	186	545	320	546	322
14	545	407	545	407	701	551	694	555
15	784	686	784	686	872	823	—a	—a
16	304	206	304	206	545	441	485	472
17	545	478	545	478	—a	—a	—a	—a
18	784	784	784	784	—a	—a	—a	—a

[a]See footnote *a*, Table IA.

[b]Approximately $66 million actually was received by Texas in production tax revenues for 1967 (see Table 4, Appendix 2). Of this amount, about $33 million came from interstate sales.

[c]Values arrived at by multiplying together tax rate, price, and quantity as determined in Table IA. For example, under conditions of line 1, revenue under the maximum tax which leaves quantity unchanged would be found by: (.359)($.192)(7,188.9), or $496 million.

[d]Values obtained by multiplying the corresponding *Total,* this table, by the *Percentage sold interstate,* from Table IA.

Table IIB

Calculated Tax Revenue from Selected Policies: Louisiana[b]
(millions of dollars)

	Maximum tax, zero quantity change		Goal 2 (maximum total revenue)		Goal 3 (maximum tax revenue)		Goal 4 (maximum interstate tax revenue)	
	$Total^c$	$Inter-state^d$	$Total^c$	$Inter-state^d$	$Total^c$	$Inter-state^d$	$Total^c$	$Inter-state^d$
1	475	395	823	690	1017	870	1015	871
2	814	704	991	863	1224	1104	1208	1098
3	1160	1041	1171	1052	1451	1366	1439	1373
4	360	296	360	296	693	533	690	536
5	589	497	589	497	834	678	832	679
6	818	707	818	707	988	840	989	843
7	322	263	322	263	585	434	578	439
8	513	429	513	429	705	554	701	558
9	704	601	704	601	835	687	833	690
10	360	304	360	304	693	605	692	607
11	589	522	589	522	834	779	829	783
12	818	761	818	761	988	972	_a	_a
13	322	269	322	269	585	478	585	478
14	513	447	513	447	705	617	704	616
15	704	639	704	639	835	772	834	773
16	322	275	322	275	585	521	880	788
17	513	466	513	466	705	679	696	685
18	704	677	704	677	_a	_a	_a	_a

[a]See footnote *a*, Table IB.

[b]Louisiana received approximately $113 million in production tax revenues, with about $90 million from interstate sales (see Table 3, Appendix 2).

[c]Values arrived at by multiplying together tax rate, price, and quantity as determined in Table IB. For example, under conditions of line 1, revenue under the maximum tax which leaves quantity unchanged would be found by: (.339)($.245)(5.7169), or $475 million. Note that the estimates for Louisiana *do not* take into account the fact that natural gas produced in the federal domain is not subject to state taxation.

[d]Values obtained by multiplying the corresponding *Total*, this table, by the *Percentage sold interstate*, from Table IA.

$690.4 million (see Table 4, Appendix 2). This total tax revenue value is exceeded by a number of the entries in Table IIB, and even the most conservative of the alternatives (maximum tax, zero quantity change) yields tax revenues exceeding one-third of 1967 revenue. Under Goal 4 every entry exceeds two-thirds of Louisiana's total tax revenue for 1967, with many exceeding the total itself. Similar comparisons can be made for Texas.

A note of caution should again be sounded: both the simplifying assumptions incorporated in the field market model and its long-run nature influence the magnitude of the results obtained in its application. Any such simple model should be interpreted most cautiously for policy purposes and should be accepted more as an indicator of a direction of change than as a predictor of magnitude of change. But, at the same time, almost regardless of the particular set of parameters assumed, these results strongly suggest that appropriate action on the part of these producing states, given a continuation of recent FPC regulatory methods, could bring sizable benefits to the taxing state. This issue will be considered further in chapter 7.

6

Optimal Tax Determination: Common Interstate Market

The assumption of a one-to-one relationship between the producing state and the interstate consuming market now will be relaxed in favor of the still very simple model where two separate gas-producing states sell to a common interstate market. This situation is analogous to the situation of Texas and Louisiana selling to the Eastern consuming regions. The intrastate markets in the respective states are assumed to be effectively isolated from one another: no gas goes interstate to be consumed within the other state. Roughly consistent with current practice, the area ceiling prices are assumed to be imposed separately in each producing state, and thus the specific tax levied in each state is added to the cost of production as determined by the FPC to form the regulated price. The further assumption is made that the ceiling prices so imposed are below the equilibrium or free-market price and, hence, that excess demand exists in the interstate market. Further generalization of the model to cases with more than two states appears possible, although difficult and tedious. In view of the obvious problems involved, no attempt was made to generalize the model further in this direction because incommensurate gain in understanding of broad directions of change was thought likely to result. Moreover, Texas and Louisiana, corresponding to the two-state model developed, together accounted for approximately 80 percent of the total interstate sales for the year 1967 (see Table 3, Appendix 2).

As discussed previously, if the regulated interstate ceiling price, P_r, is below the equilibrium price, then the supply function is the effective constraint on additional sales. Further, as shown above, all of the intrastate demand, at approximately that price, will be satisfied. Figure 13 illustrates the conditions holding in a single state where AM is the intrastate demand curve, P_r is the initial regulated price, and OQ_1 is the quantity of gas sold intrastate at that regulated price. The remainder of the gas supplied at P_r, Q_T-Q_1, will be offered for sale in the interstate market. It will, in fact, be sold there, given the existence of excess demand as posited in this discussion. Let the quantity of interstate sales, Q_T-Q_1, be designated by Q_2 (not shown on Figure 13). Increasing the state ad valorem production tax will not affect the total quantity of gas supplied as long as excess demand exists in the interstate market. However, it will result in less gas sold intrastate and more sold interstate as discussed above on pages 25-26 for the symmetric case (given excess demand) of decreasing t.

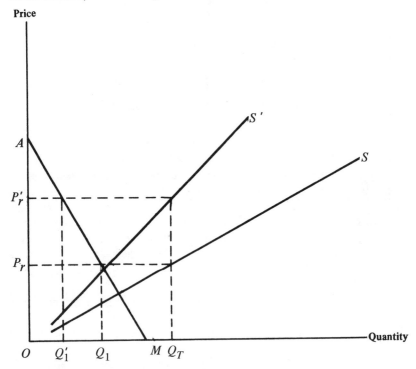

FIGURE 13

Referring still to Figure 13, a tax increase, for example, which would shift the supply curve at least up to S' and the regulated price to P_r' would bring about a decrease in intrastate sales by the state to Q_1' and an increase in interstate sales to $Q_2' = (Q_T-Q_1')$. This result would follow so long as the excess demand in the interstate market was not yet entirely eliminated by the higher price P_r' in the given state. For each such tax rate there would exist a corresponding $Q_2=(Q_T-Q_1)$. A schedule of interstate supply for this producing state thus could be drawn, valid for all those P_r such that P_r would be less than or equal to the equilibrium price in the interstate market. Shown in Figure 14,

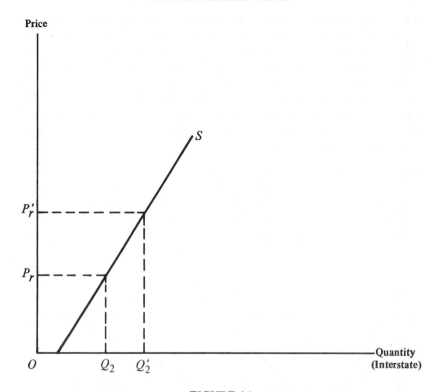

FIGURE 14

this latter schedule, corresponding to the supply and demand functions given in Figure 13, indicates by how much the hypothetical state's supply of natural gas exceeds the intrastate demand when t and hence P_r are changed. Points on this schedule corresponding to a price below the initial P_r would be obtained by reducing the production tax to zero and then making it negative by subsidizing the producers.

Two interstate supply schedules, S_A and S_B, are drawn in Figure 15 to represent that function in two different states, just as it was represented by S in Figure 14. It is assumed, for simplicity, that the same ceiling price, inclusive of production taxes, holds for both states at some initial point in time. Then the curve S_T' is a total interstate supply schedule for the two states when (under assumption) they change taxes in such a manner that equal changes in P_r result in each state.[1] The curve designated by D is the demand schedule for the single interstate market for the two states.

---

[1]There is no reason to assume that any two states would have the same underlying supply functions or the same intrastate demand functions because these may vary in

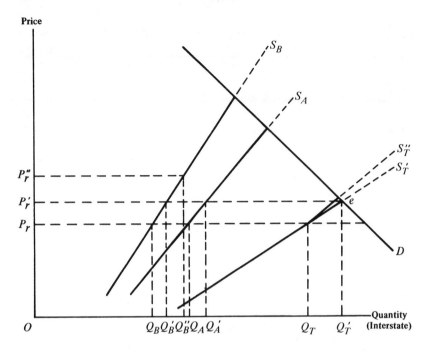

FIGURE 15

If both states raise taxes in unison just enough to eliminate excess demand, the interstate price would rise to P_r' and the quantity sold interstate would

---

different geographical and market regions. The simplifying assumption of equal regulated price, P_r, could then result from different initial levels of production taxes. In this case, equal changes in the ceiling prices, with P_r determined as on page 25, would require different tax changes in the two states. This is seen as follows:

$$C_i \quad = \quad \text{all non-production tax costs, State } i,\ i = 1,2.$$

$$P_{r_i} \quad = \quad \text{regulated ceiling price, State } i,\ i = 1, 2.$$

$$P_{r_i} \quad = \quad \frac{C_i}{1-t_i},\ i = 1,2.$$

If it is required that, as taxes are altered, P_{r_1} must equal P_{r_2}, then

$$\frac{C_1}{1-t_1} = \frac{C_2}{1-t_2}$$

or, solving for t_1,

$$t_1 = \frac{C_1}{C_2}\ (t_2 - 1) + 1.$$

increase to Q_T' along S_T'. The additional amount sold in the interstate market would come from decreased intrastate sales in both states. The quantity sold interstate by State B would become Q_B' and by State A, Q_A'. Thus, after adjustments, when both states act together to raise severance taxes up to the point where excess demand is eliminated, the total tax revenue to each state increases with the higher tax rate, revenue to producers remains the same, the proportion of gas going interstate (and tax revenue coming from interstate sales) increases, and gas consumed within the state falls, holding other factors the same. If taxes were raised beyond the point where excess demand were eliminated, some of the tax of necessity would be absorbed by suppliers.[2] With taxes at this level, given the interaction between two states, no general and unambiguous solution like the one above can be derived using these diagrams. The effects on each state would depend upon the specific values involved.

Now the effect if only one state raises its production tax may be considered. The extension of the total interstate supply function denoted by S_T'' in Figure 15, at least up to the point where it intersects D, describes the effect on interstate sales of a tax increase in State B only. It is assumed that the gas distributors or pipelines in the interstate market would buy gas from either source as cheaply as possible and under regulation then would charge a price to their customers based on the weighted average purchase price of gas. The result of the higher tax in State B is an increase in the average price of gas to the ultimate consumer, but since only a portion of the gas has its price raised, a much larger increase can be sustained in State B before excess demand is totally absorbed. In the example shown in Figure 15, State B could raise its tax to the point where the regulated price would be P_r'' so long as State A retained a tax consistent with price P_r. The quantity and price of gas sold interstate by State A would remain unchanged, as shown. Because of the different elasticity of interstate supply between State B and both states acting together, the resulting S_T'' would lie somewhat to the left of S_T' above the point of intersection with P_r. As for the intrastate effects, there would be no change at all in the quantity sold in State A; all of the additional interstate

---

[2]Perhaps a caution again needs to be sounded for the reader. This analysis ignores the process of adjustment to changes in taxes and deals only with the situation after all adjustments have taken place. In the short run (the length of which depends on such things as FPC regulatory lag, the severance tax clauses in the gas contracts, the speed of reservoir depletion), changes in taxes affect payments to factors of production and, therefore, also affect the level of output. Similarly, announcement effects of taxes may be different from their ultimate effects in practice. Further, particular pipelines and, consequently, their customers purchase gas at a limited number of locations, at discrete intervals, and under long-term contract; hence, they do not buy "average" gas, nor do they all respond in the same way. For policy interpretation, then, what is described here is a tendency over time; it is not a short-term prediction from a given action. This is simply to say that the limits of the model should be understood.

sales would come at the expense of sales to consumers within State *B*. A tax increase in State *B* beyond that which absorbed excess demand in the interstate market, of course, would affect the quantity of gas sold by State *B* Nevertheless, this higher tax well may be consistent with State *B* goals, since depending on the values for the functions, this higher tax can bring higher total revenues, tax revenues, and interstate tax revenues. Again, the quantity of gas sold by State *A,* and its interstate-intrastate distribution, would remain unchanged.

The effects of uncoordinated and non-identical tax increases by both states are identical in kind, although not degree, to a change by one state acting alone as long as the joint effect of the tax increases is not to more than exhaust excess demand. When taxes are raised beyond the point where excess demand is exhausted, then demand effects will limit gas sales in the state where the price is higher with results that cannot be predicted exactly using this regulation-influenced model. In the absence of excess demand, the usual analysis comes into play with the effect of higher prices in the competing state opening further sales opportunities for the state in question.

The main conclusions from this discussion of the two-producer-state, one-consumption-market case can now be summarized. First, without fear of retaliation, a given state can increase its taxes to form a price which, if universal, would just clear the market of the amount of gas supplied by gas producers at the resulting price to them. The consequences of adopting such a tax policy, after adjustments, would be higher tax revenue, constant producer income, higher interstate sales (and tax revenue), lower intrastate sales, but constant total sales. An even further increase in tax rates could be sustained without total sales loss as long as the other state retained its same or a lower level of taxation. The paradoxical result, then, is that under these rather special conditions of regulation a higher tax for an identical commodity can be supported in one state (without quantity effects) the *lower* the tax rate in the other state. Second, the state which has an after-tax price below the price at which the interstate market would clear, given the industry supply schedule and the regulated after-tax price to the producer, is not affected by increases in tax rates in the other state.

Thus, explicit recognition of the interdependence of two gas-producing states in a single interstate market would seem to alter the apparent opportunities for gain achieved by manipulation of the production tax by an individual state, although certainly not eliminate them. Whether Goals 2, 3, or 4 were chosen, the individual state, or the group of producing states acting together, always would benefit (or at least be made no worse off) by action taken to increase production tax to the point where excess demand was eliminated. The clear implication is that still further tax increases would be consistent with these goals under some circumstances, but this result cannot be demonstrated for the general case.

7

Conclusions and Policy Implications

The implications of the argument above can be summarized by noting that when regulation-induced excess demand for gas exists, an increase in severance taxes by the producing states sufficient to eliminate that excess demand necessarily would lead to increased state tax revenues, increased total revenues within the state, and increased gas made available to the interstate market.[1] One useful criterion for evaluating a policy of increasing the severance tax is to determine the effect this action would have on the quantity of resources commanded by particular groups. It is asserted that a policy which leads to control over more resources is preferred by a group because it leads, by definition, to the capacity to satisfy more wants (without specifying the nature of the wants involved). Using this criterion, we consider in the first two sections of these conclusions the policy implications of the analysis above. In the third section we consider an alternative open to regulation if it is determined that public policy at the federal level should discourage the producing states from exercising their potential power to shift resources from consuming states through higher severance taxes. That is, we consider (without commenting on its wisdom) a method by which federal regulators may nullify tax actions taken by the producing states in response to the original regulation itself. Finally, we conclude with brief comments on the general problem of policy formulation in an interdependent economy.

---

[1]Tax rates greater than those just sufficient to eliminate excess demand may be called for to fulfill producing state goals. For simplicity in presentation, we limit ourselves here to the conservative policy, calling attention to the fact that this is only the limiting case.

Effect of Severance Tax Increases

An increase of state severance taxes to the point where excess demand is eliminated will increase the quantity of resources controlled by a producing state. Following any of Goals 2, 3, or 4 will result in tax t', that being the tax which would shift the supply function at least to the position occupied by S' (point f) in Figure 16 and the regulated price from P_r to P_r'. Tax t' will shift a quantity of gas VL from the intrastate (AM) to the interstate (BR) market. The revenue coming into the state from foreign consumers will increase by the additional tax paid by those foreign consumers, $abfc$, and by the sales shifted away from domestic consumers, $VadL$. Intrastate consumers have lost quantity of gas VL. If for some reason it was desirable to retain those domestic consumers in the market the state could compensate them for the tax by returning to them, with some subsidy designed with the constitutional issue in mind, the tax that they would pay ($abgd$), hence maintaining intrastate consumption at L. Alternately, the state simply could compensate the intrastate consumers for their welfare loss. If a subsidy is paid to maintain domestic consumption, the revenue transfer from out of state to intrastate uses in general would be reduced, *but* still would be positive—$dgfc$.

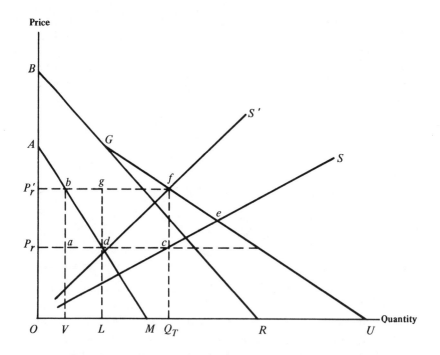

FIGURE 16

An unambiguous increase in resources controlled by the producing state thus results from raising the tax up to point f. Conceptually, no intrastate consumer is required to pay more for gas on net than he did prior to the tax increase (since the tax can be returned in the form of a higher level of services or reductions in other taxes), but the taxpayers and citizens as a whole have larger state resources to utilize for various purposes. Stated in a somewhat different fashion, an effective ceiling price confers a consumer surplus upon all consumers actually served, in this case including those outside the jurisdiction of the state. A severance tax which eliminates excess demand, as long as it is added to the regulated price, transfers that consumer surplus to the producing state where it can be used for additional social expenditures or for tax reduction and maintenance of current expenditure levels. As we have seen in chapter 6, some quantitative modifications to this conclusion are required in a two-state interactive market model, but the elements of this analysis remain correct.

To the extent that the producing state benefits from following one of Goals 2, 3, or 4, the citizens of the consuming state suffer a loss of resources devoted to their wellbeing. This loss is somewhat reduced on net because the use of a severance tax increase in an excess demand situation (up to point f) does confer an advantage upon the consuming state by substituting a market for a non-market allocation of resources, which increases the quantity of gas available to the consuming state (see below). In its negative effects, the higher tax rate transfers a consumer surplus from citizens of the consuming state to those of the producing state and reduces the total resources available to the consuming state. This burden falls on those consumers who were consuming gas before the tax was changed; these customers would be unalloyed losers if the producing state raised taxes. For the consuming state as a whole (balancing out special interests against the generality of state citizens), there is good reason to oppose any efforts of the producing states to raise production taxes in a way which would bring about a higher effective ceiling price. This result would *not* follow to the same degree if it were possible to achieve a higher ceiling price which would increase the resources available to the reproducible factors of production in the gas industry. This latter change (a higher price to producers) would lead, presumably, toward an equilibrium price which would bring higher levels of gas output and thereby reduce or eliminate any excess demand in the interstate market.

The analysis above points to an important conclusion about the current regulatory method which often is overlooked by industry regulators and by analysts: it does create a community of interest among the producing state taxing authority, the producing industry, and the producing state as an entity. It is not a case merely of special interests within the state being made better or worse off. Further, even if all of any price increase does not go to the state through changed tax *rates,* an ad valorem tax absorbs some of any increase for the state. This producing state interest in higher severance taxes is countered by a similar, but more widespread and hence less acute, welfare loss (and thus opposition) on the part of the consuming states. The FPC is caught between these two groups of political entities in administering the producer phase of the Natural Gas Act. The intergovernmental conflict resulting may grow more severe in the future.

**The Severance Tax
as an Allocative Device**

The present regulatory procedure, with the regulated price below the equilibrium price, has the common effect of all price regulating schemes: it forces nonmarket rationing. In the years before the mid-1960s, these effects scarcely were noticed nor were they particularly important in the natural gas industry. Without attempting to demonstrate the situation, it can be asserted that several factors were at work that minimized the need for overt rationing, on the one hand, and disguised what rationing did take place, on the other. First, it can be argued that the ceiling prices set by the FPC really were not restrictive through the mid-1960s. Moreover, during the 1954 through mid-1960s period of regulation the industry was running down a very excessive inventory which accumulated from discovery of gas in the search for petroleum. Additionally, the FPC, through its certification procedure, somewhat restricted the sale of gas for boiler fuel as an inferior use—still further limiting demand and postponing the day when regulated price restrictions on quantity supplied would be significant. Finally, both the pipeline industry itself and gas demand by consumers still were underdeveloped, hence the rate of output was not consistent with the long-term demand pressures which were to be felt by the end of the 1960s. In summary, the rationing requirement of an effective ceiling price was not apparent when regulation was developing within the cost-based framework.

Once this impact was felt, however, and the restriction on new supply coming forward could not be offset by drainage of inventory, the allocative effects of the ceiling price began to be noticed. Without going into the dynamics of the situation, given the supply-demand-regulated price relationships of Figure 16, gas clearly is allocated to intrastate use, which, in the absence of regulation, would go out of state. The marginal value of gas used intrastate is thus lower than the alternative use of that gas and, under the usual welfare assumptions, this allocation is inferior. Moreover, within the interstate sector allocation among potential purchasers is not subjected to a market test and, therefore, non-economic factors (implying sub-optimal allocation) serve to distribute gas among consumers. While simplistic, this approach does give a first approximation of the implications of FPC price regulation.

The current regulatory situation seems likely to lead to sub-optimal allocation. The effect on allocational efficiency of tax increases at least up to point f, therefore, might be considered. If the condition of a constant quantity Q_T is accepted, a tax rate such that the ceiling price is raised to or above point f prevents the misallocation which, as has been pointed out above, otherwise results. Both interstate and intrastate consumers are charged a price which eliminates excess demand, and only those consumers, wherever found, to whom the gas is worth this price receive it. In static neoclassical welfare terms, a tax rate consistent with P_r' generates optimal allocation of the *given* quantity of gas, Q_T, and thus in those same terms (ignoring income distribution) is preferable.

The restriction to a fixed quantity, Q_T, is a result of the ceiling price assumption. Dropping that assumption moves the analysis into the typical free market case. Again considering Figure 16, comparing the condition without regulation (e) to (P_r, Q_T), the equilibrium price would be higher, quantity would be higher, and the quantity of resources devoted to the industry would be greater. This latter situation would approach more closely the optimal allocation goal (under simplifying assumptions) of a quantity supplied and demanded where price is equal to the marginal cost of producing the commodity. The major simplifying conditions asserted to lead to this conclusion are that a competitive market exists and that the private cost of producing gas is equal to the social cost, including the opportunity cost of producing in the present rather than in the future. Both of these conditions were considered briefly above. It should be noted that, if it were concluded there was a divergence between the private and social optimal rates of exploitation, a federal severance tax (positive or negative) presumably would be the method of choice in effectuating convergence. By use of this method the allocative function of price would be used to distribute the chosen quantity of gas among competing uses, and thus the resource losses from interference with market allocation would be minimized.

**Possible Regulatory
Response to Tax Optimization**

This analysis has shown that producing states, given any one of three reasonable goals, would be better off with markedly higher severance taxes, in part because of FPC producer regulation. There are also, as demonstrated above, some benefits to be derived from the states using the tax system to bring about market allocation of the gas among competing users when excess demand exists. We have noted further that pursuit of producer state goals would reduce consumer surplus from current consumers of gas interstate and shift that surplus to the producing state taxpayers.

None of these results appear consistent with the historical position taken by the FPC, nor are they consistent with the best interests of the current interstate consumers of natural gas whom the FPC seeks to protect.[2] One matter which might be explored, then, is the response the FPC could make (or preemptively might make) to restrain producing state action designed to obtain advantage from the sub-equilibrium prices imposed on the gas industry. The FPC, should it continue to see its role as restricting the price of natural gas to interstate consumers, could announce a policy of not including any increase in severance tax in the regulated ceiling price. This action would reduce significantly the advantage to the producing state of a tax increase. Alternatively, the federal authorities simply could cease their attempt to hold the price of natural gas below its equilibrium level, accomplishing this either through explicit deregulation or through setting a ceiling price sufficiently high as not to be binding. While this effective deregulation policy is attractive on many grounds, its consideration is somewhat afield from the main thrust of this study, and it will not be discussed here.

Figure 17 demonstrates the effects of an increase in the production tax to t' when that increase is not included in the regulated price. The supply curve is shifted as before to S'. In response to this shift, the amount supplied will decrease from OQ_T to OW, this new quantity supplied determined by the intersection of P_r, the original and unchanged interstate regulated price, and S'. In contrast to the shift out of the intrastate market in the case where the increase in the tax is included in the regulated price, in this case the reduction in quantity supplied results in decreased sales in the interstate market only. This follows because failure to provide OL to the intrastate market would result in the price in this market rising above P_r, which would cause suppliers, at the margin, to shift gas from interstate customers to intrastate customers, causing price to tend again to P_r for both markets.

The effects of increasing the production tax when that tax is *not* included in the interstate regulated price can be summarized as follows:
- a decrease in total quantity supplied;
- a decrease in quantity supplied to the interstate consumers equal to the decrease in total quantity supplied as long as gas is sold in both markets;
- no effect on intrastate customers qua customers from the increase in

---

[2]One must distinguish carefully the current interstate gas consumer, who obtains his fuel at a sub-equilibrium price, from his fellow citizen, the potential interstate gas consumer who is prevented from getting gas at all because of the regulation-induced shortage. The federal policy which benefits the former usually will make the latter worse off, as he is prevented by nonmarket rationing from obtaining natural gas at a price he would be quite willing to pay. The whole issue of distributional effects of FPC producer regulation is a subject of current research by the authors.

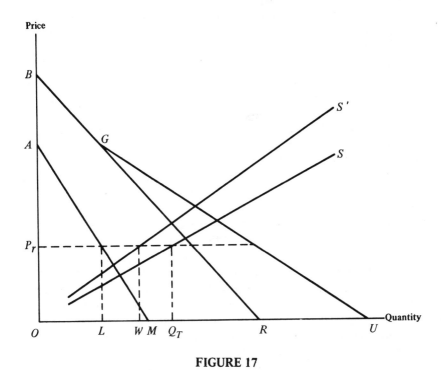

FIGURE 17

production tax as long as gas continues to be sold in both markets; and
- a decrease in total revenue (producers' revenue plus tax revenue) within the state from the sale of gas.

The economic effects on the producing state of a tax increase, should that tax not increase the ceiling price, would not be consistent with any of the state goals posited above. The incentives for state production tax increases therefore would be significantly reduced or eliminated by a federal decision that production tax changes would not be considered justification for changes in the ceiling price. It also should be noted that this policy would restrict severely the quantity of gas flowing into the interstate market if states actually increased their production taxes. This latter result has not appeared consistent with FPC policy goals either, and would represent a real threat to those goals should the states ignore the implications of an FPC warning and increase taxes despite the non-allowance policy.

Policy Interaction and Goal Conflicts

From the discussion above it is clear that there is an economic interaction between the federal regulation of the producers of natural gas and the taxing potential of the producing states. Up to the time of this writing, producing states have not embarked on a campaign of natural resource tax changes designed to exploit consuming interests. Official state activity most often has been limited to public pronouncements opposed to regulation and the regulated price, and to legal maneuverings within the regulatory context. The failure to increase severance taxes thus far can perhaps be explained by three factors. (1) Whatever the net benefits to the state from such a policy, it would require either some redistribution within the state or some rather complex adjustments which are beyond short-term political practicality. (2) The opportunities for net gain to the states from such tax changes are not obvious, and heretofore there has been little if any analysis such as that presented above to serve as a focus for public discussion. (3) The inertia factor—the time it takes to perceive and then act—has caused opportunities to be lost.

Still, the fact that in the past producing states have not sought to exploit further the tax advantages offered by the FPC regulatory method offers no assurance that they will not do so in the future. If that time comes, some serious consideration will have to be paid to alteration of the method or to abandonment of the federal attempt to hold the interstate price of gas below the market equilibrium. Just as the approaching shortfall in fuel supplies promises to reopen the whole question of the wisdom of federal regulation of natural gas producers, state tax action similarly might stimulate a reappraisal of regulation's redistributional effects.

It should not be thought that the problem we have chosen to discuss in this volume is unique, nor even that it is the most important of its type facing public policy makers today. It is, however, illustrative because the regulated industries do provide a fertile field for conflicting policy. Sometimes the divergence arises from actions taken at different levels of government, but just as often it flows from policies adopted in good faith by different agencies at the same governmental level or by the same legislative body at different times or in different contexts. Resolution of these conflicts depends in part on their recognition, and then on determination of, and agreement on, true priorities. Resolution also may depend simply on clear analysis and explicit formulation of the alternatives. This latter is the more hopeful situation; while members of a society can never expect to share totally each other's priorities, they surely can hope to make some progress toward shared understanding of the implications of given actions.

Appendix 1

Derivation of the
Combined Demand Function

The two individual demand functions are represented by

$$P = a_i + b_i Q_i, \qquad a_i > 0, b_i < 0, i = 1, 2. \tag{1.1}$$

Restricting P to be less than either a_1 or a_2, the combined demand function is obtained by summing the individual demand functions horizontally. That is, if

$$Q_i = (P - a_i)/b_i, \tag{1.2}$$

then $\quad Q_T = Q_1 + Q_2 = \dfrac{P - a_1}{b_1} + \dfrac{P - a_2}{b_2} = \dfrac{b_2(P - a_1) + b_1(P - a_2)}{b_1 b_2}$,

from which we may write

$$Q_T = \frac{P(b_1 + b_2)}{b_1 b_2} - \frac{(a_1 b_2 + a_2 b_1)}{b_1 b_2}. \tag{1.3}$$

Solving (1.3) for P, we obtain

$$P = \frac{a_1 b_2 + a_2 b_1}{b_1 + b_2} + \frac{b_1 b_2}{b_1 + b_2} Q_T. \tag{1.4}$$

Derivation of the Expression for
Elasticity of the Combined Demand Function

Prove that $\eta = \alpha_1 \eta + \alpha_2 \eta_2$, where

η = elasticity of demand of the aggregate demand function;
η_i = elasticity of demand of ith demand function, $i = 1, 2$; and
α_i = proportion of sales in the ith market, $i = 1, 2$.

Taking the derivative of equation (1.3) above, $\dfrac{dQ_T}{dP} = \dfrac{b_1 + b_2}{b_1 b_2}$.

By definition of the elasticity concept, therefore,

$$\eta = \frac{dQ_T}{dP} \frac{P}{Q_T} = \frac{(b_1 + b_2)}{b_1 b_2} \frac{P}{Q_T} \; . \tag{1.5}$$

Similarly,

$$\eta_i = \frac{dQ_i}{dP} \frac{P}{Q_i} = \frac{1}{b_i} \frac{P}{Q_i}, \quad i = 1, 2. \tag{1.6}$$

Again by definition,

$$\alpha_i = Q_i/Q_T , \qquad i = 1, 2. \tag{1.7}$$

Hence, by successive substitutions:

$$\alpha_1 \eta_1 + \alpha_2 \eta_2 = \frac{Q_1}{Q_T} \frac{1}{b_1} \frac{P}{Q_1} + \frac{Q_2}{Q_T} \frac{1}{b_2} \frac{P}{Q_2}$$

$$= \left(\frac{1}{b_1} + \frac{1}{b_2} \right) \frac{P}{Q_T}$$

$$= \left(\frac{b_1 + b_2}{b_1 b_2} \right) \frac{P}{Q_T} = \frac{dQ_T}{dP} \frac{P}{Q_T} = \eta,$$

or

$$\eta = \alpha_1 \eta_1 + \alpha_2 \eta_2. \tag{1.8}$$

Appendix 2

TABLE 1

Natural Gas Production and Revenues, Major Producing States, 1967

State (1)	Marketed production[a] MMMcf (2)	Percentage of total (3)	Cumulative percentage (4)	Gas sales revenue[a] ($000) (5)	Percentage of total revenue (6)	Cumulative percentage (7)
Texas	7,188.90	39.56	39.56	948,935	32.74	32.74
Louisiana	5,716.86	31.46	71.02	1,057,619	36.48	69.22
Oklahoma	1,412.95	7.78	78.80	202,052	6.97	76.19
New Mexico	1,067.51	5.87	84.67	138,776	4.79	80.98
Kansas	871.97	4.80	89.47	116,844	4.03	85.01
California	681.08	3.75	93.22	202,290	6.98	91.99
Wyoming	240.07	1.32	94.54	35,051	1.21	93.20
West Virginia	211.46	1.15	95.70	50,962	1.76	94.96
Others	780.53	4.30	100.00	146,211	5.04	100.00
Total	18,171.33	100.00	—	2,898,741	100.00	—

[a]*Minerals Yearbook*, 1967, Vol. I-II, Table 2, p. 759.

TABLE 2

Non-Factor Costs in Gas Price at the Wellhead, 1967

State	Average value at wellhead^a (¢/Mcf)	Production tax^b (¢/Mcf)	After tax royalty^e (¢/Mcf)	Lease Bonus^f (¢/Mcf)	Non-factor costs (¢/Mcf)	Non-factor costs (percentage) (6) ÷ (2)
(1)	(2)	(3)	(4)	(5)	(6)	(7)
Texas	13.2	0.9^c	1.7	0.5	3.1	23.5
Louisiana	18.5	2.3	2.3	0.4	5.0	27.0
Oklahoma	14.3	0.7^c	1.9	0.6	3.2	22.4
New Mexico	13.0	1.0^c	1.6	0.4	3.0	23.1
Kansas	13.4	0.0^d	1.9	0.6	2.5	18.7

^{a}*Minerals Yearbook*, 1967, vol. I-II, Table 2, p. 759.

^{b}The values of the production taxes were obtained from a questionnaire sent directly to the respective states' offices of taxation. The tax rate for New Mexico varies slightly from one school district to another, hence the 8 percent figure is only approximately correct.

^{c}Converted from ad valorem rates as follows: tax (¢/Mcf) = (average value at wellhead) x (ad valorem rate).

^{d}Tax is between 0.0025 and 0.0050 cents per Mcf. "The statute provides no definite amount of tax, and the Commission is empowered to tax according to the extent of its budgetary requirements." Docket No. AR 64-1, *Joint Initial Staff Brief*, vol. 1, 31 May 1967, pp. 247-48.

[e]Converted from percentage rates as follows: After-tax royalty in cents per Mcf = [average value at wellhead ($¢$/Mcf) - production tax ($¢$/Mcf)] x royalty (%). Royalty percentages and sources:

Texas, 13.5 percent. This is an arithmetic average of royalties pertaining in three producing regions: Texas Gulf Coast, 14 percent; Hugoton-Anadarko, 14 percent; and Permian Basin, 12.5 percent. *Presiding Examiner's Initial Decision on Texas Gulf Coast Area Rates,* Docket No. AR 64-2 (16 September 1968) p. 156; *Presiding Examiner's Initial Decision on Hugoton-Anadarko Area Rates,* Docket No. AR 64-1 (16 September 1968) p. 146; *Opinion No. 468, Opinion and Order Determining Just and Reasonable Rates for Natural Gas Producers in the Permian Basin,* Docket No. AR 61-1, p. 66.

Louisiana, 14 percent. Based on a figure in *Opinion No. 546, Opinion and Order Determining Just and Reasonable Rates for Natural Gas Producers in the Southern Louisiana Area,* Docket No. AR 61-2, p. 60.

Oklahoma, 14 percent. Based on *Hugoton-Anadarko,* p. 146.

New Mexico, 12.5 percent. Based on *Permian Basin,* p. 66.

Kansas, 14 percent. Based on *Hugoton-Anadarko,* p. 146.

[f]Lease bonus figures were obtained by using one-half of estimated lease acquisition costs, rounded to the nearest tenth of a cent. The estimates used were as follows:

Texas, 1.01 $¢$/Mcf, obtained as an arithmetic average of lease acquisition costs in three producing regions (1.13 $¢$/Mcf, *Hugoton-Anadarko,* p. 49; 0.76 $¢$/Mcf, *Permian Basin,* p. 51; and 1.13 $¢$/Mcf, *Texas Gulf Coast,* p. 52).

Louisiana, 0.76 $¢$/Mcf, *Southern Louisiana,* p. 36.

Oklahoma, 1.13 $¢$/Mcf, *Hugoton-Anadarko,* p. 49.

New Mexico, 0.76 $¢$/Mcf, *Permian Basin,* p. 51.

Kansas, 1.13 $¢$/Mcf, *Hugoton-Anadarko,* p. 49.

TABLE 3

Natural Gas Interstate Shipments and Production Tax Revenue, 1967

State (1)	Marketed production[a] (MMMcf) (2)	Proportion of marketed production shipped interstate[b] (3)	Quantity shipped interstate[b] (MMMcf) (4)	Production tax[c] (percent) (5)	Interstate production tax revenues[d] ($000,000) (6)
Texas	7,188.90	0.484	3,479.43	7.0	32.150
Louisiana	5,716.86	0.800	4,573.49	12.4	90.464
Oklahoma	1,412.95	0.560	791.25	5.0	5.658
New Mexico	1,067.51	0.740	789.96	8.0	8.215
Kansas	871.97	0.573	500.00	0.0	0.000
Total	16,258.19	–	10,134.13	–	136.487

[a] *Minerals Yearbook*, 1967, vol. I-II, Table 2, p. 759.

[b] Beginning with the 1966 *Minerals Yearbook* gas produced in one state and exported to another is not tabulated separately. All gas leaving a state is listed as "Interstate Movements, Deliveries," regardless of the state of origin. The quantities listed in column (4) in this table are estimates based upon the proportion of gas produced in each state which was shipped to other states for the years 1961 to 1965, this fraction [column (3) above] being applied to marketed production data in the 1967 *Yearbook*.

[c] The values of the production taxes were obtained from a questionnaire sent directly to the respective states' offices of taxation. The tax rate for New Mexico varies slightly from one school district to another, hence the 8 percent figure is only approximately correct. The ad valorem tax rate given for Louisiana was converted from the actual 2.3 cents per Mcf rate which that state imposes.

[d] Obtained by multiplying column (3) this table by column (4) of Table 4.

TABLE 4

Natural Gas Production Tax as Proportion of Total State Tax Revenue, 1967

State	Value of marketed production^a ($000,000)	Production tax^b (percent)	State production tax revenue ($000,000) (2) x (3)	State total tax revenue^d ($000,000)	State production tax revenue (percentage) (4) ÷ (5)
(1)	(2)	(3)	(4)	(5)	(6)
Texas	948.935	7.0	66.425	1,335.8	5.0
Louisiana	1,057.619	12.4	113.080^c	690.4	16.4
Oklahoma	202.052	5.0	10.103	401.0	2.5
New Mexico	138.776	8.0	11.102	205.8	5.4
Kansas	116.844	0.0	0.000	355.2	–
Totals	2,464.226	–	200.710	2,988.2	–

^{a}*Minerals Yearbook*, 1967, Vol. I-II, Table 2, p. 759.

^{b}See footnote *c*, Table 3; footnote *d*, Table 2.

^{c}For Louisiana account must be taken of the fact that gas production from federal offshore areas is not subject to state production tax. Data for Louisiana production on the outer continental shelf for fiscal years 1958-1966 would seem to indicate that about 14 percent of gross Louisiana production fell in this category (*Petroleum Facts and Figures*, 1967 edition, pp. 54, 55, 66). Hence the figure for marketed production in column (2) was multiplied by a factor of 0.86 before multiplying by the 2.3 cents per Mcf production tax in obtaining the tax portion of the entry in column (5).

^{d}*Facts and Figures on Government Finance*, 15th Biennial Edition, 1969, pp. 170-171.